IN SEARCH OF
PARADISE
GREAT GARDENS OF THE WORLD

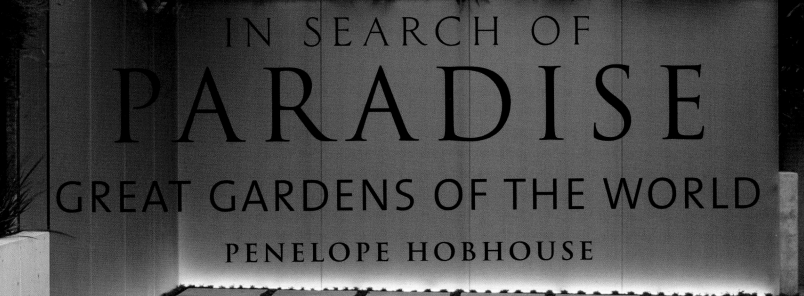

IN SEARCH OF
PARADISE
GREAT GARDENS OF THE WORLD

PENELOPE HOBHOUSE

F

FRANCES LINCOLN LIMITED
PUBLISHERS

in association with

CHICAGO BOTANIC GARDEN

Frances Lincoln Limited
4 Torriano Mews, Torriano Avenue
London NW5 2RZ
www.franceslincoln.com

Chicago Botanic Garden
1000 Lake Cook Road
Glencoe, Illinois 60022
www.chicagobotanic.org

In Search of Paradise:
Great Gardens of the World
Copyright © Chicago Botanic Garden 2006

This book was published in conjunction
with the dedication of the
Joseph Regenstein, Jr. School
of the Chicago Botanic Garden, 2006

First Frances Lincoln edition 2006

A catalogue record for this book is
available from the British Library.

Printed and bound in Singapore

ISBN 10: 0 7112 2615 6
ISBN 13: 978 0 7112 2615 9

9 8 7 6 5 4 3 2 1

PAGES 2–3
Oliver Garden, San Francisco,
California. Designed by
Topher Delaney for Steve and
Nancy Oliver, 1996
RIGHT
Shute House, Dorset, England.
Designed by Sir Geoffrey
Jellicoe for Michael and
Lady Anne Tree, 1969–88

CONTENTS

GARDENS TODAY

FOREWORD

In spring 2002 I was excited to be asked by Barbara Whitney Carr, President and Chief Executive Officer of the Chicago Botanic Garden, to be the visiting curator for an exhibition entitled *In Search of Paradise: Great Gardens of the World*, which was to open in January 2003. The intention was to present world garden history in the most accessible way, using modern photography to show how iconic gardens look today and old engravings, drawings and paintings to trace their historical development. This was a compelling prospect for me, as it offered an opportunity to explore the dialogue between culture and nature in gardens over the centuries; for the ideal garden is at the balance point between human control and untamed nature.

In spring 2005 the Chicago Botanic Garden, as part of an extensive building and educational program expansion, decided to revive the original concept of *In Search of Paradise*. The new exhibition would emphasize contemporary gardens, including modern designs that stressed an ecological and environmental approach almost unknown to previous generations. Although garden design principles are global, the most successful modern gardens give high priority to their regional settings and the needs and habits of native plants.

It was also decided to produce a book that would be both a record of the two exhibitions and an account of gardens through the centuries, from the oldest known gardens to the most recent designs.

While I was working on the first exhibition I was also completing my book on the *Gardens of Persia,* which dealt with the origins of the desert garden, both in the centuries before Islam, and after the seventh century as a metaphor for Paradise. The vital element in these early gardens was water, without which there could be no shade trees, no orchards and no sustenance. Through the centuries, and still today, water, in all its moods, whether ample or scarce, has remained the most important ingredient in gardens. This becomes very evident as one moves through the exhibition at the Chicago Botanic Garden and the pages of this book. In the first section, "Gardens Through the Centuries," old progresses to new, as bubbling fountains worked by gravity in the deserts of Persia give way to baroque exuberance at Peterhof, then to eighteenth-century naturalism at Stourhead, and to the refined layouts and water-saving systems of today.

A garden needs to express man's affinity with the natural world, to expand nature's potential and not to harm it. The section called "Gardens Today" illustrates the designer's role in reconciling aesthetics with an appropriate respect for nature. The final garden presented is the extraordinary Garden of Cosmic Speculation, in which Charles Jencks has introduced a new scientific language of garden design while using nature to speculate on deeper ideas.

As we worked on the exhibitions and the book, it became evident that they were a celebration not only of gardens, but also of garden photography. Susan Boothe of Chicago Botanic Garden has been indefatigable in her search for superb pictures which outshine any possible written descriptions. Modern garden photography has reached a level at which it measures up to the work of the great painters of landscape. Skilled in technique and sensitive to the changing forms of shadow and sunlight, photographers capture the beauty of gardens through the seasons and at every time of day, but particularly at the magic moments of dawn and twilight. Those photographers who truly understand the philosophy behind the designer's vision produce the finest portrayals of the garden landscape – as the following pages reveal.

ACKNOWLEDGMENTS

Susan Boothe of Chicago Botanic Garden has been the guiding spirit behind the two *In Search of Paradise* exhibitions and this book. Many other members of Chicago Botanic Garden staff have contributed to the project, including: Paula Johnson, photo procurer and administrative assistant; Karen Zaworski and Lee Randhava, copy editors; Leora Siegel and Carol Line, library staff; and Roger Vandiver, exhibition designer. At Frances Lincoln, editor Jo Christian and graphic designer Becky Clarke shaped the exhibition script and images into the format of this elegant publication.

Evening Island via the Serpentine Bridge, Chicago Botanic Garden. Evening Island designed by Oehme, van Sweden, & Associates, Inc., 2002.

GARDENS THROUGH THE CENTURIES

The story of garden design threads together four thousand years of cultural history and personal vision. Throughout history gardens have been refuges and sanctuaries; records tell of their abundance, comfort and beauty. From the oldest known gardens to the most recent designs, garden-making has offered evidence of humankind's ongoing search for Paradise.

IN THE BEGINNING

The earliest gardens were oases in the deserts of the Middle
East. Other early gardens were recorded in the river cultures
of Mesopotamia and Egypt. Even as early as 2000 BC, the
waters of the Euphrates, Tigris and Nile rivers were
irrigating pleasure gardens as well as crops.

Water, the very spirit of life itself, can transform even the
most hostile setting. Many of the world's great gardens,
some hundreds of years old, are famous for the ways in
which they harness the power of water.

THE PARADISE GARDEN

As recorded in the Old Testament – the scripture common to Judaism, Christianity and Islam – the Garden of Eden was identified with Paradise. In the seventh century, Muslims expanded this theme into terrestrial gardens. Intended to be a foretaste of the celestial Paradise to come, these gardens were laid out in four parts divided by water rills, or channels. The idea of a Paradise Garden spread to Spain in the eighth century and to India with the Mughals in the sixteenth century.

Tomb of Nebamun

Egyptian tomb paintings give us the earliest known portrayals of gardens in Western civilization. Created to accompany the deceased on the long journey through the afterlife, the paintings most likely represent existing gardens of the time. This painting in the tomb of Nebamun (c. 1400 BC) shows a water tank with fishes and birds and an orchard where tree goddesses lurk.

Bagh-e Shahzadeh

Although it was built in the nineteenth century, the Bagh-e Shahzadeh evokes the sense of the very earliest gardens, which were walled enclosures that provided protection from marauders and shifting sands. A dramatic aerial view shows the classic layout, with pavilions at each end. Water cascades down a central slope flanked with flower beds and tall plane trees.

Babur's Garden of Fidelity

The first Mughal Emperor Babur (1483–1530) was interested both in garden layouts and in flowers. His memoirs, the *Babur Nama*, were illustrated with miniature paintings, as shown here. One of his gardens, the Garden of Fidelity near Jalalabad, is a *chahar-bagh*, or four-part layout, divided by water rills with a central pool. It is typical of early Paradise Gardens.

Bagh-e Fin

Kashan, Iran. Built by the early Safavids, 1590

The Bagh-e Fin may have existed as a garden long before it was developed by the great Shah Abbas. It is the oldest living garden in Iran. Water arrives here from the mountains via underground conduits known as *quanats*. Stored in a reservoir, water is gravity-fed throughout the site.

The layout, an extension of the symmetrical fourfold plan characteristic of the Muslim Paradise Garden, opens out in a series of rectangular compartments. Turquoise-lined pools with bubbling fountains flow into wide basins aligned across shallow terraces, while four-hundred-year-old cypresses create shade and mystery along the walkways.

RIGHT
Taj Mahal
Agra, India. Built by Shah Jahan for his wife, 1632–43
The Taj Mahal was built on the south bank of the River Yamuna by Shah Jahan as a mausoleum for his wife, Mumtaz Mahal. The building stands on a raised terrace, overlooking the garden to the south and a more distant garden (now being restored) on the north bank. The actual garden is a vast *chahar-bagh*, a four-part area crossed with waterways, with a central channel and fountains. This layout is typical of developments of Persian garden style that took place in India under the Mughal emperors.

PAGES 20–21
Bagh-e Shahzadeh
Mahan, Iran. Designed by Naser ad-Douleh, 1880s
The walled enclosure at Shahzadeh is a typical Muslim garden, with a central water channel and irrigated orchards – a green oasis in the hostile desert environment. Although planting was minimal, trees were important for both shade and sustenance. The vital element, water, was brought from the mountains by underground conduits, then stored in reservoirs.

The Court of the Lions

Alhambra, Granada, Spain. Built by Nasrid caliphs, 1370–90

The fourteenth-century Court of the Lions is a rectangular courtyard in the
Alhambra complex. Along with the adjacent Court of the Myrtles, it was
the last garden to be made by the Moors in Spain. The enclosed space is divided
by water rills into four equal quadrants. The central fountain is supported by
stone lions, from whose mouths water flows into the surrounding basin. From
there the water is channelled under carved stucco porticoes that provide shade
and a place to linger.

ASIA

*The garden designs of China and Japan
reflect a reverence for nature rather than
a mastery of it. Gardening is considered
a partnership with nature.*

*From earliest times, Chinese emperors created
vast panoramic gardens. Later, scholarly
mandarins found peace in secluded gardens
where each rock's placement had meaning.*

*In Japan, an affinity with nature extended to the
first pleasure gardens. By the fourteenth century,
secluded enclosures in Japanese gardens provided
places for contemplation; stroll gardens and
moss gardens were later developments.*

CHINA

HAVENS FOR RETREAT

The earliest emperors constructed huge pleasure parks for hunting and for growing rare
fruits and trees imported from the far reaches of their empires. Later, Chinese mandarins built
smaller gardens as intellectual havens for retreat. These gardens were constructed
as miniaturizations of the landscape with rocks representing mist-wreathed mountains
and water pools suggesting lakes.

Yuan Ming Yuan

The first complete description of a Chinese garden
available in Europe was published in 1749. It
described Yuan Ming Yuan, the Emperor Ch'ien
Lung's garden outside Peking, as the "garden of
perfect brightness." The garden included audience
halls, courtyards, pavilions, grottoes, contoured hills
and valleys, trees and winding streams. All were
laid out as if by chance, in total contrast to the
ordered design of European gardens. This painting
by T'ang Tai and Shen Yuan (1744) depicts one of
forty views of the garden.

BELOW
Lan Su Yuan

This classical Chinese garden, called Lan Su Yuan or Garden of Awakening Orchids, opened in Portland, Oregon, in September 2000. It contains the five elements essential to a Chinese scholar's garden: water, stone, architectural details, literary references and plants. The buildings represent the ordered thought of the Confucian doctrine, while the landscape expresses the Taoist view of chaotic nature. Rocks represent ancient mountains; water invites contemplation; pavilion windows provide glimpsed views; and poetic inscriptions hint at deeper meanings.

PAGES 28–29
Liu Yuan
Suzhou, sixteenth century

The Chinese word for landscape is *shanshui*, meaning "mountains and water." At Liu Yuan, or Garden to Linger In, rocks represent mountains and the masculine quality of *yang*. Water represents the opposite – but complementary – female quality of *yin*.

Rocks were valued elements in the great imperial landscapes, and suitable stones were much sought after. Lake Tai, near Suzhou, was the source of prized water-worn specimens. At Liu Yuan, the desired irregularity in design was achieved with a twisting entrance passage and winding walkways.

JAPAN

THE CONTEMPLATIVE GARDEN

The contemplative gardens of Japan, many laid out during the Muromachi period (1393–1568), are based on the Zen Buddhist philosophy that was originally imported from China. They achieve a sense of simplicity through an economy of materials, while demonstrating a belief that the cultivation of beauty has a profound spiritual significance. Representing a natural landscape of mountains and cliffs, a dry Zen garden is composed entirely of rocks and gravel. Each rock is placed to contribute to the whole design. Gravel or sand is raked or brushed to resemble ocean waves.

Zuiho-in

The Zuiho-in garden in Kyoto is the supreme example of the *kare sansui* or dry Zen garden. It is an idealized landscape in which rocks and raked gravel symbolize the ocean. Zen Buddhist philosophy encouraged priests to discover the ultimate meaning of such arrangements through intense meditation. In this way, the cultivation of beauty becomes a profoundly spiritual experience.

RIGHT
RIGHT
Daisen-in

The Daisen-in garden in Kyoto was laid out in the
Muromachi period by Kogaku Shuko (1464–1548). It
was composed in the tradition of Chinese Song
paintings, with a three-dimensional miniaturized
landscape of rocks, cliffs, shrubs and cascading water.
Water, represented by gravel, flows under stone
bridges, around islands and over a dam.

BELOW
Kinkaku-ji

Built in Kyoto at the end of the fourteenth century,
Kinkaku-ji, the Temple of the Golden Pavilion (now
known as Rokuon-ji), was the retirement home of the
Ashikaga Shogun Yoshimitsu. The garden was
designed to be viewed from a slowly moving boat,
so that the subtle reflections of the building and
twisted pine trees would be revealed. Along the
perimeter, small trees and rocks representing
mountains make the garden appear larger. The whole
garden shows the distinct influence of Chinese
landscape painting.

PAGES 32–33
Ryoan-ji

Kyoto. Designer unknown, possibly designed by Soami, 1450

Enclosed by earthen walls, the garden at Ryoan-ji Temple in Kyoto, known as the Garden of
Crossing Tiger Cubs, was created at the end of the fifteenth century. Except for some moss
around the rocks, no plants are used. Fifteen rocks are arranged so that from any point of
view one rock remains hidden.

PAGES 34–35
Tenryu-ji

Kyoto. Designed by Muso Kokushi for Shogun Ashikaga Takauji, 1339

The talented priest Muso Kokushi constructed a pond at Tenryu-ji that emulates the
Chinese Song landscape painting style. In Japanese garden ponds, a rock in the shape of a
crane or tortoise symbolizes longevity and alludes to the legendary Isles of the Chinese
Immortals, where everlasting life might be found.

Kinkaku-ji

Kyoto. Built by Ashikaga Shogun Yoshimitsu, late fourteenth century

The garden of Kinkaku-ji, the Temple of the Golden Pavilion, features early blooming cherry trees and azaleas that cover the wooded slopes with color in the spring. The still water acts as a mirror for the glimmering building. When viewed from a path along the lake's perimeter, the calm reflections are broken up by craggy rocks and islands.

THE STROLL GARDEN

Japanese garden philosophy – in which beauty does not depend on the flowering habits of plants – has not always been understood in the West. Stroll gardens, which were developed in the seventeenth to nineteenth centuries, relied on plants to evoke a sense of place. Landowners created paths that led visitors on "excursions" through their properties, where famous landmarks, natural features, or even lines of poetry or literary stories were expressed symbolically in careful compositions of trees, shrubs, rocks and water.

Stroll gardens exemplified the principles of *shakkei* – "hide and reveal" and "borrowed scenery."

Honshu Island

On Honshu Island in Kyoto, a stone path fringed with moss leads to a small pavilion on the temple grounds, from which a miniaturized landscape can be observed. As in the ritualized tea ceremony, each element along the stroll path is carefully placed so as to encourage an appreciation of the spiritual world.

PAGES 40–41

Saiho-ji

Kyoto. Designed by Muso Kokushi, 1339

The garden of Saiho-ji has survived for nearly a thousand years. It was conceived as the earthly representation of the paradise surrounding the Buddhist deity Amida. Restored and improved by the priest and artist Muso Kokushi in 1339, this stroll garden appears to have no boundaries, with forests of bamboo and wooded hills leading to endless vistas. The famous moss garden appeared spontaneously during a period when the Buddhist monks could not take care of the garden.

PAGES 42–43

Ritsurin Park

Shikoku. Designed by the Takamatsu branch of the Matsudaira clan, 1670s–1744

The Ritsurin, once a private estate of the Matsudaira lords, is now a public park. In the Edo period (1603–1867) *daimyo*, aristocratic military lords, began to build large gardens such as this. It is a typical example of a Japanese stroll garden, with views at first hidden and then revealed on the lake path. A graceful bridge, a pavilion, and the "borrowed scenery" of the surrounding forests are all reflected in the still water, creating a scene that looks like a landscape painting.

CONTINENTAL EUROPE

Renaissance humanists transformed Italian gardens. Looking to classical Greece and Rome for inspiration, they introduced the architectural concepts of balance and symmetry as organizing principles. Many of their gardens survive, providing a grammar of design still valid today.

By the sixteenth century, Italian ideas had spread to France where, in a flatter landscape, garden designs became more linear. The baroque exuberance of late seventeenth-century French gardens became the inspiration for many gardens throughout Europe.

ITALY

Renaissance architects found inspiration in both Roman ruins and classical literature.
They developed a love and reverence for nature completely alien to the medieval mind. The inward-
looking garden of the Middle Ages turned outward to take advantage of its surroundings.
Writers recommended siting gardens for the views and the invigorating air. The first Renaissance
gardens, arranged axially to a villa, were simple expressions of cubic and geometric space,
but by the seventeenth century they had became more baroque, with bulging stonework
and extended perspective views.

Villa Lante

The Villa Lante in the Lazio was created for Cardinal
Gambara by the architect Vignola, in the 1560s. The
perfect geometric hillside garden, it is divided into
a series of vignettes in which sunlight and shadow,
sculptural stone carving and a spectacular water
parterre all contribute to unity of design. The
cascade, a long rivulet shaped like a series of
elongated *gamberi*, crayfish, to celebrate Cardinal
Gambara, flows down the center of the garden.

Villa d'Este

Pirro Ligorio began work on the Villa d'Este in Tivoli in 1559, at the behest of Cardinal d'Este. The steep descending terraces, laid out on a grid system, provided a perfect setting for elaborate and theatrical water features. The Rometta, pictured here, is a semicircular stage on which the city of Rome, with its seven hills, is represented in miniature, while fountains spray from the stone boat that appears to float in the pond.

Villa Medici at Pratolino

This statue by the Flemish sculptor Giambologna is all that remains to remind a visitor of this garden's glory. Designed in the late sixteenth century by Bernardo Buontalenti for the Grand Duke Francesco, the garden was famous for its innumerable grottoes and music-making hydraulic automata. The colossal figure, representing the Apennine mountains, presses his hand down on a monster's head, from which water gushes.

PAGES 48–49
Hadrian's Villa

Tivoli, Lazio. Designed by the Emperor Hadrian, AD 118–138

Erected by the Emperor Hadrian, this villa is a vast complex on the plain near Tivoli. Many of its architectural and decorative aspects – open porticoes, enclosed atriums, fountains, basins and statuary – were inspired by classical features. The pool shown here took its inspiration from the Canopus in Egypt. Ancient Roman gardens such as this influenced Italian Renaissance garden design, which in turn influences today's gardens.

RIGHT
Villa Medici at Castello

Castello, Tuscany. Designed by Nicolo Tribolo
for Grand Duke Cosimo I de' Medici, 1537

At the Medici villa at Castello, a country orchard was transformed
into a sophisticated geometric garden that included a collection of
lemon trees and a cypress maze. Allegorical statues celebrated the
power of the Medici family in Florence. The figures of Hercules and
Anteus symbolized victory over tyranny, while Venus symbolized
eternal spring – both allegories of the family's rule in the city. The
garden's most interesting feature was the Grotta degli Animali,
its walls decorated with animals saved from the Flood
and marble basins carved with garlands of shells and fishes.

PAGES 52–53
Villa Orsini

Bomarzo, Lazio. Designed by Vicino Orsini, 1552–1564

The park at the Villa Orsini at Bomarzo, known today as the Sacro
Bosco, bears little resemblance to the ordered gardens typical of the
period. It is strewn with grotesque allegorical stone monsters
derived from mythical, heraldic and literary sources. Count Orsini
found inspiration in the works of Virgil and Dante as well as in those
of the contemporary poet Ludovico Ariosto. The Hell Mask, a huge
gaping mouth, which is the entrance to a banqueting hall, bears the
inscription:

> *Lasciate ogni pensiero voi ch'entrate.*
> Abandon all thought, you who enter here.

This phrase substitutes *pensiero* (thought) for *speranza* (hope) in a
line from Dante's *Inferno* describing the mouth of hell.

VILLA GAMBERAIA

The gardens of the Villa Gamberaia, at Settignano in Tuscany, date to the early seventeenth-century design of Zanobi Lapi, although few details of its original appearance survive today. The water panels were introduced at the turn of the nineteenth century, when the garden was restored by the Romanian Princess Giovanna Ghyka. The four pools and the hedged arcades frame a view of the city of Florence below. Together with the original features, they form a matchless ensemble of perfectly arranged proportions.

LEFT
Lemon Garden

Reached by a double staircase from the *giardino segreto*, this garden contains a collection of lemons in ornamental terra cotta pots, which are overwintered in the large *stanzone*. Citrus fruits were often grown in Italian Renaissance gardens, and many different varieties of lemons, citrons and oranges were available. More than two hundred different forms of sweet lemon were grown in the sixteenth-century Medici gardens.

BELOW
Water Parterre

The water panels were introduced at the end of the nineteenth century by Princess Ghyka and her companion, Miss Florence Blood. Upright yew topiaries, boxwood hedging, clipped mock privet and cypress arcades frame the view to the River Arno and Florence in the valley. Although the reconstruction was not authentic, the garden conveys a strong feeling of the Renaissance.

PAGES 56–57
Giardino segreto

The *giardino segreto* – enclosed garden – at the Villa Gamberaia is overhung with trees that provide welcome shade in summer. This garden probably dates to the early seventeenth century, although much of the decoration has been restored over the centuries. The walls are ornamented with mosaic pebbles, while elegant balustraded staircases lead to the lemon garden above. The statues on the walls and balustrades probably date to later garden restorations.

La Mortola

Liguria. Created by the Hanbury family owners, 1867–present

The famous Hanbury garden at La Mortola on the Italian Riviera, now known as the Giardini Botanici Hanbury, has steep slopes descending to the sea. Planting first began here in 1867. Both native and exotic desert succulents, agaves, aloes and cycads cling to the upper slopes, while roses, salvias, tender vines and citrus fruit grow below. Eucalypts and melaleucas from Australia, cypresses from Mexico and scented acacias all thrive in the Mediterranean climate.

FRANCE

The French, borrowing Renaissance ideas from Italy, found it difficult to establish geometric gardens aligned on central entrances around their medieval-styled châteaux. By the seventeenth century, however, symmetrically shaped buildings had given French landscape architect André Le Nôtre the opportunity to design formal gardens on a grand scale. Vast water features and tricks of optical illusion control the viewer's perception. The French baroque garden, exemplified by Versailles with its parterres and clipped plants, became a model for all the courts of Europe.

Le Roman de la Rose

This Flemish illustration for *Le Roman de la Rose* (c. 1485) shows an enclosed garden of the Middle Ages beside the castle walls. It contains the typical features of a medieval pleasure garden: trelliswork divisions, a central fountain, raised flower beds, orchard trees and a turf bench. Here the Lover wanders in the outer garden until he is let in by Idleness and finds himself in a place full of joy.

RIGHT
Le Grand Trianon

From the 1660s until his death in 1715, Louis XIV was constantly enlarging the palace and garden at Versailles to demonstrate his power and serve as a visible symbol of his concept of French monarchy. Aided by André Le Nôtre,

the greatest gardens in the world, with paths flanked by

hing toward the horizon. Le Grand Trianon,

g by Jean-Baptiste Martin, lies to the north of

nce. Designed by André Le Nôtre

–61

es the French linear approach to garden design and t in perspective and hidden features. Built for Louis ux-le-Vicomte incorporates dramatic changes of reciated only by visiting the garden and moving rolled parterres, clipped yews and fountains.

Designed by André Le Nôtre for Louis XIV, 1661–1715 ntain of Apollo with the Château of Versailles in the e Nôtre aligned the main axes of the garden on the e long perspective view from the Grande Galerie across es into the setting sun. Although water was an sailles, the actual water supply brought from the Seine ufficient, so gardeners had to turn fountains on and off grand progress through the garden.

signed by Constant d'Ivry échal de Belle-Isle, c. 1740 u de Bizy a gently sloping canal descends smoothly eps. Hardly a ripple disturbs the silence as the water e dolphins. Beyond the dolphins, a magnificent stone garden surrounded by balustrades in the cour ard. Water moves quietly and elegantly here. The ts as a visual path that leads the visitor into the

LEFT
Château de Groussay
Montfort l'Amaury, Île-de-France. Redesigned by Charles de Beistegui, *c.* 1938
The Château de Groussay near Paris was built in 1825 for the Duchesse de Charost. The gardens were much altered and expanded by Charles de Beistegui, who became the château's owner in 1938. In this romantic, naturalistic setting, water mirrors the trees and the bridge; here, the day's mist and open sky turn the lake into a pool of light in the foreground. The garden beautifully illustrates how still water can double dimensions and give the illusion of greater space.

PAGES 70–71
Giverny
Giverny, Île-de-France. Designed by owner Claude Monet, 1883–1926, pond built 1895
Monet's famous paintings of water lilies were made in his own garden at Giverny, just north of Paris, where he lived and worked from 1883 until his death in 1926. His garden was an extremely personal one and was the main inspiration for many of his later paintings. Both the water garden, dappled with spreading waterlilies, and the elegant Japanese bridge, curtained in wisteria, are familiar and beloved subjects of Monet's work. The water garden was carefully restored in the 1980s.

GERMANY

Schwetzingen

Baden-Württemberg. Designed by J. Ludwig Petri, Friedrich von Sckell and others for the Electors Palatine, eighteenth century

Many European gardens originally planned in the French baroque style were later adapted to incorporate an English landscape park, while retaining their formal elements. The outer areas of Schwetzingen were redesigned by Friedrich von Sckell in the English landscape style, from 1786. He reshaped the rectangular pools to give them irregular outlines and introduced buildings including a Turkish mosque and the Temple of Apollo (shown below). The garden has been restored to show the transition between the two opposing ideals. The parterre (shown left) was reconstructed in 1974 to the original design by J. Ludwig Petri.

NETHERLANDS

Het Loo

Apeldoorn. Designed by Daniel Marot for William and Mary, 1690s
The Palace of Het Loo, originally a hunting lodge, was expanded for
William III, King of England and Prince of Orange, and his wife, Queen
Mary, in the 1690s. Although indebted to Versailles in its axial layout,
ornamental parterres and sculptures depicting classical subjects, Het
Loo is designed on a more intimate scale. Flattened to make way for
an English garden in the eighteenth century, the grounds have
recently been authentically restored, as has the palace.

RUSSIA

BELOW

Tsarskoe Selo

St. Petersburg. Designed for Catherine I, Empress Elizabeth and
Catherine the Great by various architects, including Jan van Rosen, John
Busch, Vasily Neyelov and Charles Cameron, eighteenth century

The original formal garden at Tsarskoe Selo outside St. Petersburg,
renamed Pushkin after the Bolshevik Revolution, has recently been
restored. The garden was originally laid out in the 1700s by Dutch
architect and designer Jan van Rosen in French baroque fashion, with
wide terraces decorated with flower beds. It was extended for the
Empress Elizabeth after the 1750s. Later, Catherine the Great introduced
the English style in the south and west of the park.

RIGHT

Peterhof

St. Petersburg. Built for Peter the Great by various architects,
including Jean-Baptiste Alexandre Le Blond, Niccolo Michetti and
hydraulics expert Vasily Tuvolkov, 1714–23

One of the world's most famous water gardens frames Peter the
Great's palace Peterhof (also called Petrodvorets) on the Gulf of Finland.
Water is the organizing principle of this garden. It tumbles down
marble steps, blasts from numerous fountains, and then settles into a
quieter canal that leads to the nearby Baltic Sea.

The pool's central statue of Samson portrays him overpowering a lion,
from whose jaws a jet of water shoots high into the sky. Almost
totally destroyed during the Second World War, the garden has been
entirely re-created.

ENGLAND

As England emerged from its medieval past, garden design was dominated by Italian and French formality. However, in the early eighteenth century a new relationship with nature led to a revolution in design. Naturalistic landscapes, no longer dependent on geometry, came to influence future garden designs throughout the world.

In Victorian England, a return to formalism saw annuals bedded out for spectacular effects. In contrast, Edwardian gardens, while still structured, often contained relaxed cottage-style planting. This style lasted through the twentieth century.

THE LANDSCAPE GARDEN

The eighteenth-century English landscape garden developed from contemporary ideas in poetry, philosophy and painting and a more democratic political ideal. It expressed an understanding and appreciation of man's partnership with the natural world. It was also a reaction to the rigid control practiced in seventeeth-century French gardens. In place of geometry, with its mirror-image *allées* of trees and clipped plants, the English style introduced contoured land shapes and sinuous curves of grass and water. Groves of trees and parkland were often separated from the surrounding countryside by an invisible fence called a ha-ha.

Stowe

The landscape at Stowe in Buckinghamshire was constructed between 1715 and 1779. Three famous designers were involved: Charles Bridgeman, William Kent and Lancelot "Capability" Brown, working for Viscount Cobham, Earl Temple and the first Marquis of Buckingham. A series of temples, a Palladian bridge (shown here), busts of worthies, canals and luxuriant naturalistic valleys turned the estate into a romantic Arcadian paradise typical of the new landscape style. Some of the themes demonstrated political opposition to the ruling Whig government.

LEFT
Hampton Court

This painting, *A View of Hampton Court* by Leonard Knyff, shows the gardens after completion under William and Mary, at least thirty years before the earliest naturalistic English landscape gardens of the 1730s. Charles II had introduced the *patte d'oie* (avenues radiating from a central point, in a shape that suggests a goose foot) and a central long canal. In 1689 Daniel Marot established the Great Fountain Garden, with its scrolled parterres, fountains, statues and topiaries.

PAGES 82–83
Painshill

Surrey. Designed by owner Charles Hamilton, 1738–73

Charles Hamilton, an enthusiastic amateur gardener, planned his naturalistic landscape park at Painshill in Surrey between 1738 and 1773. His landscape design interpreted different moods with appropriate buildings and planting schemes. Included were a Temple of Bacchus, mock ruins, an elaborate grotto, a rustic hermitage, a Chinese bridge and the Gothic Tower, viewed here from across the lake. Hamilton was particularly interested in acquiring trees and shrubs newly arrived from America to incorporate into his naturalistic landscapes. Facing financial ruin through overspending, he sold Painshill in 1773. The garden and many of the buildings have recently been restored.

PAGES 84–85
Stourhead

Wiltshire. Designed by owner Henry Hoare II, 1745–70s

Stourhead, created by the talented banker and landowner Henry Hoare II, is among the earliest landscape gardens in England. Devoid of straight lines and clipped trees, the landscape, including a lake, woodland slopes and classical temples, represents a new relationship between man and nature, and specifically between the amateur "improver" and his property. This view of Stourhead includes the Palladian bridge and Pantheon seen across the lake, which was created by damming the River Stour. The result is a light-filled scene, reminiscent of a pastoral landscape painting by Claude Lorrain.

PAGES 86–87
Chatsworth

Derbyshire. Designed by London and Wise, Capability Brown, Jeffry Wyatville and Joseph Paxton, from the seventeenth to nineteenth centuries, for the Dukes of Devonshire

At Chatsworth the formal gardens date to the last years of the seventeenth century. But by the 1760s Capability Brown, the most famous of the mid-eighteenth-century "improvers," had been called in by the fourth Duke of Devonshire to landscape the parkland in the new naturalistic style. Although the great French-type avenues of trees were cut down to make way for a lake and groves of trees (typical of Brown's design style), much of the original inner garden was retained. Today naturalistic landscape and formal gardens, enhanced by Joseph Paxton's Victorian additions, sit happily side by side.

Studley Royal

North Yorkshire. Designed by owner John Aislabie, 1722–42

This fine, formal water garden is a geometric arrangement of lakes, canals and the famous reflecting Moon Pools – one round and one crescent-shaped. The sky, the surrounding woods and the beautiful Temple of Piety are all reflected in the pools. Built more than two hundred and fifty years ago, this remains one of England's most important water gardens.

Studley Royal epitomizes early eighteenth-century English design just before the more naturalistic styles were introduced. The garden is the work of John Aislabie, who, after a disastrous ending to his political career, retired to his family estate and devoted his remaining years to his gardens.

THE COTTAGE-STYLE GARDEN

In the late nineteenth century, William Robinson advocated a return to more natural plantings. In *The Wild Garden*, published in 1870, he recommended the use of hardy garden plants in self-perpetuating communities, rather than the extravagant bedding out of annuals. His disciple Gertrude Jekyll, working with the architect Edwin Lutyens, orchestrated highly colored border themes into works of art. Together they created many gardens that were typical of the cottage style: a mixture of shrubs, perennials, bulbs and annuals, all arranged inside a strong structure of walls and hedges, showing a nostalgia for the past.

Sissinghurst Castle
At Sissinghurst Castle in Kent, during the 1930s, Vita Sackville-West and her husband, Harold Nicolson, turned a ruined farm with handsome brick walls into a twentieth-century masterpiece of design and planting. Nicolson laid out the architectural framework, leaving his wife to do the imaginative planting in a series of garden "rooms." Sissinghurst has become an icon for sophisticated cottage-style planting.

Barnsley House

Rosemary Verey's garden at Barnsley in Gloucestershire was inspired by historical layouts and embellished with cottage-garden planting schemes that expressed her own color and plant preferences. Her laburnum walk is underplanted with alliums and with hostas that grow up to replace them through the summer months. Verey's designs in Europe and the United States have influenced many of today's gardeners.

RIGHT
Gravetye Manor
Sussex. Designed by owner William Robinson, 1885

Gravetye Manor, the home of William Robinson, prophet of natural gardening, became a mecca for his disciples. The modern restoration of Gravetye Manor shows Robinson's relaxed style, with billowing borders of a variety of roses, shrubs and perennials, all flowering in profusion.

PAGES 94–95
Hestercombe
Somerset. Designed by Edwin Lutyens and Gertrude Jekyll
for E.W. Portman, 1906

The gardens at Hestercombe were created in 1906 by the celebrated partnership of Edwin Lutyens and Gertrude Jekyll. The epitome of the Edwardian garden, Hestercombe is considered their joint masterpiece. Lutyens's stone framework – terraces, steps and rills, in addition to the giant pergola – holds Jekyll's cottage-style plantings together. Drifts of silver-leaved plants link the border with aromatic lavender at the base of the wall.

PAGES 96–97
Sissinghurst Castle
Kent. Designed by owners Vita Sackville-West and Harold Nicolson, 1930s–62

The White Garden at Sissinghurst is dominated by the great rambling *Rosa mulliganii* on the arbor. Formal boxwood hedging, groups of spiky-leaved irises and silver-foliaged plants contribute to the garden design.

The gardens at Sissinghurst Castle were based on cottage-style plantings in the mode of Lawrence Johnston at Hidcote Manor and the color themes of Gertrude Jekyll. Sissinghurst, today owned by the National Trust, is one of the most visited gardens in England. Its naturalistic mixed plantings, contained by a strong underlying structure, appeal to many modern gardeners.

THE ECLECTIC GARDEN

During the nineteenth century, technological advances, plant introductions and the diffusion of knowledge through gardening magazines and horticultural societies led to much experimentation in the garden. The gardens at Biddulph Grange in Staffordshire, begun in the 1850s by the orchid expert James Bateman, with the aid of marine artist Edward Cooke, provide an outstanding example of the eclectic gardening style. The gardens had an extraordinary framework of individual compartments – including a pinetum, a rhododendron area, a "stumpery," a rocky glen and an avenue of Himalayan cedars and wellingtonias – in which exotic plants from all over the world were displayed in appropriate settings.

"China"

Most exciting of all the compartments at Biddulph Grange is a section called "China," reached through a rock tunnel. A red-painted temple overlooks a lake surrounded by Chinese plants. East Asia had only recently been opened up to plant explorers, and the Wardian packing case made plant transportation back to England possible.

"Italy"

This view of the Italian garden shows its recent restoration by the National Trust. Irish yews and conifers, backed by large mounded evergreen shrubs, show a design scheme typical of the many Italianate gardens constructed in the Victorian period. Elsewhere, James Bateman made a parterre of monkey puzzles (*Araucaria auracana*), whose seed was introduced from Chile in 1844.

"Egypt"

In "Egypt," the theme is reinforced by stone sphinxes and a tomb entrance flanked by yew hedges trimmed as obelisks and backed by a yew pyramid. A tall beech hedge along the eastern terrace conceals the Egyptian court from the rest of the garden to ensure an element of surprise. Inside the pyramid a statue represents the Ape of Thoth, associated by Egyptians with the study of botany.

PAGES 100–101
"The Glen"

While other Victorian landowners were investing in glasshouses for rearing annuals for seasonal bedding, James Bateman's great interest was in utilizing new plants in appropriate settings, both cultural and horticultural. In one of the rocky dells, he created favorable microclimates and soil conditions for different types of plants. Bateman collected ferns, rodgersias and gunneras, which thrive in this damp site.

NORTH AMERICA

The gardens of the seventeenth-century European settlers in North America were enclosures firmly fenced against the incursions of nature, and laid out in the simple geometric patterns then standard in Europe. Throughout the eighteenth century, the majority of gardens remained formal in design. Only in the nineteenth century, as Americans began to appreciate the beauty of the unspoiled wilderness, did the naturalistic landscape garden come into vogue. By the beginning of the twentieth century, the early environmentalists were already expressing awareness of threats to native plants as they searched for suitable regional gardening styles.

EUROPEAN INFLUENCES

The first gardens in seventeenth-century America were adaptations of European gardens that consisted of fenced enclosures with geometric layouts. During the eighteenth century, gardens remained essentially formal, expanding to grand box-edged affairs containing both exotic and native plants. By the early nineteenth century, Americans were developing a new appreciation of their own countryside and they began to lay out parks and cemeteries in the more natural style inspired by the English landscape ideal.

Middleton Place

The most opulent eighteenth-century gardens were located in the South, where the mild winter climate allowed experimentation with new plants. On the Ashley River near Charleston, South Carolina, Henry Middleton employed Englishman George Newman to build his garden. Newman worked from 1741 to 1751. The curved terraces and butterfly ponds (part of Newman's ingenious water system for rice growing), *allées* and a grand canal show the influence of the European baroque.

Filoli

Filoli, William Bourn II's garden in Woodside, forty miles south of San Francisco, contains all the axial compartments of an Italianate garden. Filoli's walls and hedges mark out its geometric components. A narrow *allée* of Irish yews, broken by steps to adjust levels, stretches up a southern slope. The yews (*Taxus baccata* 'Fastigiata') are cuttings from Muckross Abbey, a Bourn property in Ireland.

Vizcaya

The most imposing Italian-style garden in America, Vizcaya is located on Biscayne Bay in Florida. Designed for James Deering by Diego Suarez and F. Burrell Hoffman between 1912 and 1916, Vizcaya echoes the gardens of Villa Lante and Gamberaia. Suarez's elaborate Italianate gardens, with their extravagant stonework and gushing fountains, were truly grand creations, even for the opulent Gilded Age.

PAGES 106–107
Middleton Place

Charleston, South Carolina. Designed by owner Henry Middleton, 1741
Although Middleton Place was laid out with formal elements in the eighteenth century, much of the planting is extremely naturalistic. Both native and exotic plants were used to blur the straight structural lines of the garden – a new idea for the time. Middleton Place is dominated by live oaks dripping with Spanish moss and by swamp cypresses that flourish in the wetter areas.

PAGES 108–109
Filoli

Woodside, California. Designed by Bruce Porter for William Bourn II, 1916
The manicured gardens of Filoli (an acronym for "fight, love, live") were designed as a series of geometric "rooms." Regional plantings take advantage of the mild climate. With its irrigated emerald lawns, Filoli has the ambience of an oasis, a defiant contrast to the arid surrounding countryside. It is the most beautiful formal garden in America.

PAGES 110–111
Dumbarton Oaks

Washington, D.C. Designed by Beatrix Farrand for Mildred Woods Bliss, 1921–47
Beatrix Farrand, one of the first successful women landscape designers in the United States, studied the proportions and symmetry of the gardens of Italy. She was also aware of Arts and Crafts principles, having studied the relationship of modern design to the past. Farrand's gardens integrate classical influences with regional plantings. On the steep wooded slopes of Dumbarton Oaks, a series of descending terraces, flanked by massive plantings of cherries and forsythia, create a mixture of formal and informal – a triumph of ingenuity.

PAGES 112–113
Stan Hywet

Akron, Ohio. English Garden redesigned by Ellen Shipman for Gertrude Sieberling, 1928
Warren Manning, among the earliest American naturalistic designers, created the main garden features of Stan Hywet around several formal elements, including the English walled garden. This garden, a private space for the owner's wife, was redesigned by Ellen Shipman in 1928. Shipman used lush plantings around the central pool to soften the formal architecture.

Naumkeag

Stockbridge, Massachusetts.
Designed by Fletcher Steele.
Cascades built 1938–9

The gardens around the Choate family's 1870s house near Stockbridge were redesigned by landscape architect Fletcher Steele, with the enthusiastic help of Mabel Choate, who inherited the house in the late 1920s. The famous blue "cascades," framed with elegant arches and terraced steps, are fed from an upper water channel. The water collects in four deep pools before continuing its way down the hillside. White-painted railings echo the vertical trunks of the paper birch trees that flank the steep slopes. This iconic view remains Fletcher Steele's acknowledged masterpiece.

THE NATURALISTIC GARDEN

By the early nineteenth century, American gardeners were beginning to adopt more naturalistic
gardening ideas. They were influenced by Andrew Jackson Downing's books on landscape theory,
which encouraged garden design that reflected the beauty of the unspoiled landscape.
Toward the end of the century, American designers promoted gardens that expressed democratic
values, with unfenced front lawns uniting suburban properties. Early environmentalists, such as
Jens Jensen in the Midwest, pressed for regional garden styles in which native plants were
used in preference to those that were imported.

Mount Vernon

George Washington was
already familiar with Batty
Langley's *New Principles of
Gardening* (1728) when he
designed a pear-shaped
entrance lawn for Mount
Vernon in Virginia. Langley
championed gardens with
winding paths and sinuous
curves in place of rigid
geometry. Although both the
upper flower garden and the
lower vegetable garden at
Mount Vernon were laid out
geometrically within
encircling walls, the
vegetable area, shown here,
was raised above the field
level to provide Washington
with a view to his much-
prized Virginia woods.

RIGHT
Central Park

Central Park in New York City, today an oasis surrounded by towering skyscrapers, was designed by Frederick Law Olmsted and Calvert Vaux, beginning in 1858. Influenced by parks he had seen in England, Olmsted created an area in the city with natural features and plantings. He incorporated the peculiar characteristics of the site, using the marshy ground and rocky outcrops to extend his theme. Olmsted's idea of providing "green lungs" for city dwellers has been adopted throughout the world.

LEFT
Winterthur

At Winterthur in Delaware, Henry Francis du Pont first began to turn a family property into an extraordinary naturalistic garden in 1927. His use of spring ephemerals such as May apples, Virginia bluebells and trilliums inspired many American gardeners to copy his endeavors. Drifts of pink and white azaleas grow under the natural canopies of tall tulip poplars.

JENS JENSEN GARDENS

Jens Jensen, originally from Denmark, worked for the Chicago Park District as well as for private clients. An advocate of naturalistic landscapes, Jensen considered the natural topography and the historic use of a site in his designs. He preferred broad, flowing lines rather than the straight lines that he associated with the traditional garden geometry of autocratic European society. Jensen's designs are characterized by the use of native stone, prairie trees planted in groves, curving pathways and broad expanses of slow-moving water that allow fringe plantings of native perennials.

Columbus Park
Stonework

Jensen excelled in designing stonework to resemble the irregularities of the natural limestone bluffs found along the Illinois, Rock and Mississippi rivers, where stratified rock flanks the deep river channels. One of his most successful commissions was for the 144-acre Columbus Park on the western boundary of Chicago. He worked there between 1915 and 1920, designing a landscape of waterfalls surrounded by groups of trees, stepping-stone paths and meadowlike plantings of wild flowers and native shrubs. The waterfalls appear to emerge from a natural spring and cascade into the meandering lagoon, which Jensen called a "prairie river."

Columbus Park
Pathways

Jensen used local stone to create paved pathways, placing stones irregularly for an informal feeling. Often the paths curve out of sight around a group of hawthorn or crab apple trees. Jensen installed a series of berms to separate park areas, such as the outdoor stage – the Players' Green – and, a signature Jensen design element, the council ring.

PAGES 120–121
Edsel and Eleanor Ford House
Grosse Point Shores, Michigan. Designed by Jens Jensen for Edsel and Eleanor Ford, 1926–32

Edsel and Eleanor Ford encouraged Jens Jensen's belief in native plantings and in using the natural features of the landscape. At the Fords' garden outside Detroit on the shores of Lake St. Clair, sugar maples and American elms curve around an open sunlit meadow, oriented toward the setting and rising sun. Far from the formal geometric designs and the grand "country place" gardens of the turn of the century, Jensen's naturalistic designs are particularly suitable for large-scale gardens and public parks.

Columbus Park
Prairie River

Columbus Park's meandering lagoon simulates the prairie rivers of the Midwest. Emerging from the rocky bluffs, the broad, slow-moving water – a feature found in many of Jensen's landscapes – runs through an ancient beach depression. The banks are planted with moisture-loving wildflowers and occasional groups of native trees and shrubs. In 1930 Jensen wrote that he considered Columbus Park to be his most successful interpretation of the native landscape of Illinois.

PAGES 122–123
Lincoln Memorial Garden
Springfield, Illinois. Designed by Jens Jensen for the Garden Club of Illinois, 1936

For his most memorable commission, the Lincoln Memorial Garden, Jens Jensen chose an undeveloped site on the shores of Lake Springfield. Its gentle slopes and little hills and valleys provide a perfect setting for native plants. Open glades are surrounded by woodland, wildflowers grow on the lake shore, and a circular council ring serves as a meeting place. The garden, an inspiration to environmentalists and ecologists, is an important part of Jensen's legacy.

GARDENS TODAY

The best contemporary gardens are informed and inspired by the great gardens of the past, but make use of new ideas, materials and technologies. They express the creative visions of their owners and designers, yet are firmly connected to nature. The plants in these gardens are chosen for environmental reasons, as well as for their intrinsic beauty.

The search for Paradise continues.

WATER IN THE GARDEN

Today's private and public gardens often feature elaborate waterfalls, streams, cascades and fountains. These are made possible by technical advances in hydraulics and the use of computerized controls. Self-contained, recirculating water systems are now embraced as a solution to the twin issues of environmental responsibility and water scarcity.

Water's powers of reflection and movement continue to inspire today's garden designers, just as they have done in the past.

WATER'S MANY MOODS

Water has always been used to create illusions and inspire reactions. Channelled or expanded, calmed or agitated, water can create contrast and surprise. In the seventeenth century, the Italians devised *giochi d'acqua* (water games) to amuse garden visitors, who were often astonished – and soaked – by the tricks that water could play. Today's garden designers employ hydraulic technology to evoke a range of moods from jocular to contemplative.

Cascade, Alnwick

The grand French-style cascade with serpentine walls in the garden at Alnwick Castle, Northumberland, England, is the creation of Belgian designer Jacques Wirtz. Water tumbles over steps on a steep slope, descending to bubbling pools and arching water jets. Every half hour, spectacular fountains shoot into the air. Underground tanks provide storage; elaborate computer-driven devices ensure adequate water pressure. The design is reminiscent of the famous water pergolas at the sixteenth-century Garden of Miracles at Pratolino in Italy.

Woollahra Garden

Originally from Czechoslovakia, Vladimir Sitta now works mainly in Australia, creating ultra-modern designs. He believes that gardens should be intimately associated with their surroundings and he often uses water as the connecting medium, as in this garden for a private residence in Woollahra, New South Wales, Australia. A water rill that runs alongside the path to the front door is a calm presence juxtaposed with the dynamic hardscape of rhomboids and rectangles.

PAGES 130–131
Auckland Garden
Auckland, New Zealand.
Designed by Ted Smyth, 1981

Garden designer Ted Smyth has long admired the Mexican landscape architect Luis Barragán. Like Barragán, Smyth uses a limited number of elements in his designs. By setting these elements against broad planes of water and sky, he produces strongly architectural forms.

In this garden's pool, small water-controlled jets define the space, but it is the softly underlit rectangular arches that draw the eye. They frame views to the garden, the sky and the countryside beyond. A large dragon tree sits alone in black cobblestones.

Surrey Garden

Surrey, England. Designed by Graham Pockett and Andrew Wilson, 2002
Sunlight and shadow create the spatial illusions that give this garden its
constantly changing appearance. Islands of smooth lawn appear to float on the
infinity pool, while the black surface reflects the crisply rendered walls and
umbrella-shaped privets. Seen through the break in the wall, the natural
landscape of dark pines, birches and rhododendrons contrasts sharply with the
garden's controlled geometry.

The simple and practical use of concrete slabs, grass squares and flat water is
architectural and thought-provoking.

Les Quatre Vents

Quebec, Canada.
Designed by owner
Francis Cabot,
1975–present

At Les Quatre Vents, on
the St. Lawrence River,
Francis Cabot has created
a vast garden in which
he incorporates themes
and ideas from many
cultures and countries.
Here, the Pigeonnier is
modeled on a French
barn Cabot saw during
his travels. The
rectangular canal,
flanked by eastern cedar
hedges and panels of
lawn, acts as a mirror,
effectively duplicating
the building and its
irresistible archway.
Passing through the arch,
the canal broadens into a
wide pool, carrying the
eye into the Laurentian
landscape and beyond.

Town House Court

Sydney, Australia.
Designed by
Vladimir Sitta, 1993

Vladimir Sitta believes
that his gardens should
be a refuge from the
practicalities of everyday
life. In this townhouse
courtyard, minimal
elements and materials
– a reflecting water
channel, bamboos and
mondo grass – give the
garden a Japanese
simplicity. The calm
space provides peace for
contemplation, and
despite the courtyard's
diminutive size,
the garden has a
powerful presence.

LEFT
Welch Sanctuary
Woodinville, Washington. Designed by owner Terry Welch, 1978–present
Terry Welch's design reinterprets Japanese tradition in an unexpected location – the Pacific Northwest of the United States. His garden reflects the philosophy that he developed during time spent in Japan, where he visited Zen Buddhist sites that represented the surrounding topography in miniature. His *kare sansui* – or dry garden – includes low rocks that suggest islands, tall rocks that cast long shadows, and raked gravel that mimics ocean waves.

Where water itself cannot be present, its suggestion can still be a powerful force in the garden.

PAGES 138–139
Piet Boon Garden
Oostzaan, the Netherlands. Designed by Piet Oudolf, 2001
The garden designed for Piet Boon, one of the leading architects of the Netherlands, by Dutch plantsman and designer Piet Oudolf demonstrates Oudolf's extraordinary knowledge of grasses and their ability to work successfully in formal spaces. Here, Oudolf masses soft, billowing golden tufted hair grass to create powerful forms. The grasses, with their spectacular golden yellow seed heads, are juxtaposed with a raised central canal that reflects the sky and clouds.

In this garden, water is used simply and architecturally. Its presence challenges the viewer to consider which surface is hard and which is soft.

PAGES 140–141
Camp Sarch
Minorca, Spain. Designed by Fernando Caruncho, 1989–90
The Arab presence in Spain, from the ninth to the fifteenth centuries, left a Moorish influence that continues to inspire architecture and garden styles throughout the Iberian peninsula. Spanish landscape architect Fernando Caruncho admits to a strong Moorish-Hispano influence in his designs, though he also sees his gardens as reinterpretations of broader classical ideals.

At this vacation home in Minorca, Caruncho used the outlines of the garden that previously existed here, which was possibly Moorish. He designed a grid of five pools surrounded by clipped mounds of evergreen escallonia. Deceptively simple at first glance, the design details of the pools, with their varying pitches and water levels, are immensely complicated.

ECOLOGICAL GARDENING

A simple definition of ecological gardening is the practice of matching plants to appropriate sites in the landscape. Many of today's gardeners, however, are choosing to garden ecologically at an even more fundamental level. They are installing native or non-hybrid plants instead of new varieties. They are planting in the rhythmic patterns of nature instead of forcing formality. And they are proponents of biodiversity, water conservation, and chemical-free gardening.

Every gardener becomes the keeper of their land. Practicing ecological gardening helps ensure the health of the land for the next generation.

FOLLOWING NATURE'S LEAD

Beth Chatto was the first nurserywoman to encourage an awareness of plants' needs, habits and natural habitats. Her writings have helped gardeners everywhere understand how soil conditions dictate the selection of site-appropriate plants. The Beth Chatto Gardens and Nursery in Essex, England, have become a mecca for all serious gardeners.

Damp Garden

Chatto credits her ecologist husband, Andrew, with teaching her the importance of ecological gardening – that is, using appropriate plants for the site. In her Damp Garden, built around a spring-fed lake, Chatto chose moisture-loving shrubs and perennials that enjoy wetter conditions. Creeping willows, ferns and yellow flag iris all thrive along the shore.

RIGHT
Woodland Garden

The latest area of Beth Chatto's garden to have been completed is the woodland. Flowers carpet this garden in late winter and spring. In this photograph, taken in late spring, species peonies and bright blue columbines mingle with sweeps of pale blue forget-me-nots; as the canopy of oaks overhead starts to fill in, shade-tolerant perennials will take over. Chatto has systematically cut back trees to create pockets of light and open air, and to contrast with areas of deeper shade.

LEFT
Gravel Garden

Beginning in the early 1990s, Chatto transformed the dry, gravelly, compacted site of an old parking lot into one of the best-known gardens in England. Her Gravel Garden has achieved iconic status.

Arranging drought-resistant plants in abstract patterns, Chatto encouraged self-seeders for a more natural look. In late summer, site-compatible plants such as grasses, tall, upright mulleins and the pale giant sea holly known as Miss Willmott's Ghost continue the naturalistic theme.

Right Plant, Right Site

Today's designers embrace the idea of using site-appropriate plants – that is, native plants or those that will thrive in the soil of that particular site. The talent for placing the right plant in the right spot has become as valuable as the talent for making sophisticated color schemes. The garden designer's skill lies in understanding not only what is beautiful, but also what is ecologically desirable.

Van Sweden Garden

James van Sweden is a partner in Oehme, van Sweden & Associates, Inc., a landscape architecture firm that is known for its meadowlike designs of massed grasses and North American prairie plants. Van Sweden often designs for public spaces, but here he has created an understated garden at his private domain on Chesapeake Bay, on the coast of Maryland. The planting is simplified and overtly natural, with indigenous grasses and reeds used to great effect.

BELOW
Old Rectory

In order to be sustainable over a long period, successful ecological designs depend on choosing plant neighbors that thrive in similar conditions. At the Old Rectory in Sussex, England, garden designer Christopher Bradley-Hole has raised beds to varying levels on the sloping site. These accommodate golden grasses and tall verbenas, which require good drainage, and joe-pye weed, which needs richer, deeper soil.

PAGES 148–149
Wigandia

Noorat, Victoria, Australia. Designed by owner William Martin, 1990–present
Artist William Martin explores the complex relationship between landscape, environment and society. In his own garden on Mt. Noorat in the dry bush of western Victoria, where rainfall is very low (just thirty-one inches annually), he uses only drought-tolerant, stress-adapted plants from similar climates. Here, spiky agaves and spear lily grow under trees such as the dragon tree. The garden is named for *Wigandia caracasana*, a hardy native that is covered with stinging hairs.

PAGES 150–151
Home Farm

Northamptonshire, England. Designed by Dan Pearson, 1987–2001
Dan Pearson's design for Home Farm incorporates his firm belief in creating distinct, site-specific environments, informed by an acute "sense of place." Although his work is highly aesthetic, he believes in working with nature, rather than trying to manage and manipulate it. He also believes in choosing appropriate plants for a site rather than creating unnatural conditions for a particular plant.

At Home Farm, yew mounds anchor the naturalistic mix of stipa grasses, mulleins, self-seeding giant sea holly, poppies and oxeye daisies.

Bury Court

Surrey, England. Designed by Piet Oudolf and Christopher Bradley-Hole for owners Marina Christopher and John Coke, 2001 and 2002

LEFT Piet Oudolf's design philosophy was inspired by Karl Foerster, a 1930s German nurseryman. Foerster encouraged a naturalistic and ecological style of perennial planting, which Oudolf has made his signature.

At Bury Court, he divided the space into different themed areas. The enclosed yard, dominated by old oast houses, was once the site of a midden. Now the space is occupied by a small gravel garden, two perennial borders, a modern knot garden and, in semi-shade, a meadow of pale hair grass.

BELOW Christopher Bradley-Hole makes good use of silhouetted trees and a new pavilion in the front garden at Bury Court. Like Piet Oudolf, Bradley-Hole selects his plants for their appropriateness to the site. In this calm scene, an axial path is flanked by elegant, waving grasses that draw the eye up the slope to the natural landscape beyond.

RIGHT

Valentine Garden

Santa Barbara, California. Designed by Isabelle Greene with owner
Carol Valentine, 1980–84

Acclaimed landscape architect Isabelle Greene designed the Valentine garden
in Santa Barbara with water conservation in mind. One of the first xeriscape
(dry landscape) designers, Greene used native California plants such as spiky
agaves, aloes and yuccas, as well as plump succulents and silver-leaved plants.
These require no supplementary watering, even in drought years.

The design of the Valentine garden is a joint effort of owner and designer;
they call the style "California Zen" for its sympathy with the state's water-
scarcity challenges.

PAGES 156–157

RHS Garden Wisley

Surrey, England. Designed by Piet Oudolf, 2001

At the Royal Horticultural Society's garden at Wisley, Piet Oudolf created two
vast new borders in 2001. Each 482 feet long and 36 feet wide, the parallel
borders include a backdrop of shrubs and an *allée* of dogwood. Amending the
soil allowed Oudolf to introduce North American perennials suitable for the
English climate. Coneflowers and sweeps of tall grasses ensure meadowlike
effects and late-autumn interest.

Wisley, visited by countless RHS members during the year, is a showcase for
ecological gardening principles.

BOTANIC GARDENS

Public botanic gardens are great educational resources. They are generally designed with ecological principles in mind – that is, they display indigenous plants or plants that have adapted to the surrounding environment. These two botanic gardens – Kirstenbosch, in the mountains of South Africa, and the Desert Botanical Garden, in the Arizona desert – are in very different natural settings. However, both promote the principles of ecological gardening. In these grand public spaces, visitors can learn about regional, native and endangered plants – and those that may thrive in their own gardens.

Kirstenbosch National Botanic Garden

Set in a natural wooded area on the eastern slopes of Table Mountain in South Africa, Kirstenbosch focuses entirely on native flora, with an emphasis on the unique indigenous plants of the Cape region. The garden is a public learning resource that promotes education, conservation and the importance of using site-specific plants. It displays at least 50 percent of the local indigenous plants, as well as one quarter of the twenty thousand plant species native to South Africa.

Desert Botanical Garden

Set among sparse vegetation and red rock outcrops in the Sonoran Desert, the Desert Botanical Garden in Phoenix, Arizona, displays plants from dryland regions around the globe. Its cactus collection, with more than 1,350 different varieties, is considered one of the most comprehensive in the world. In this view of the garden, saguaro cactus (*Carnegiea gigantea*), an Arizona native with a columnar form, towers over agaves, succulents and prickly pear.

NATURE IN THE CITY

Frederick Law Olmsted believed that his design for Central Park, proposed in 1858, would provide the people of New York City with a public space in the heart of the city. Calling the park "the lungs of the people," Olmsted envisioned its green meadows, wooded groves and calm lake as places of recreation for hard-pressed city workers.

Central Park was not the first city park, but it fostered the idea of a green oasis in an urban area. In recent years there has been an explosion of plans for turning run-down urban areas into places with grass, trees and flowers. Cities are responding to the growing public demand and providing outdoor green spaces, from modest neighborhood gardens to Chicago's grand new Millennium Park (shown at right).

RECLAIM & REVITALIZE

Public spaces in an urban environment bring enjoyment and beauty to city dwellers. Because undeveloped urban space is at a premium, "brown field" sites have become a valuable resource. These former industrial areas can take on a new life when developed imaginatively, with due regard to environmental issues.

Land reclaimed as public space need not be grand in size – even the smallest pocket garden can add a new dimension to daily city life.

Parc André Citroën

The Parc André Citroën, in southwest Paris, opened in 1992. With grand open areas, intimate color-themed gardens, jet fountains and pathways, it revitalized a run-down suburban district. Created by the talented designer Gilles Clément, it is on the site of an old Citroën automobile factory. Here, a sunken area is designed with a formal pattern of trees and shrubs, all planted in gravel.

Landschaftspark

The German landscape architect Peter Latz specializes in the revitalization of blighted industrial areas. At Duisburg-Nord, a densely populated area of the Ruhr, between 1991 and 1999, he transformed an iron production factory into a city park where each year half a million visitors enjoy alpine climbing gardens, a diving center and viewing towers. Latz encourages "volunteer" plants, which have naturally developed in the depleted soil of the slag.

Bonnington Square

The pleasure garden in Bonnington Square in south London was created from an old bomb site, a remnant of World War II. In 1990 local residents, many with careers in the arts, banded together as the Bonnington Square Garden Association to design the garden. The small, sheltered site has a semitropical climate that allows for a wide range of plants, from palm trees to drought-resistant silver-leaved perennials.

RIGHT

Atocha Station

Madrid, Spain. Designed by
Rafael Moneo, 1992

The total overhaul of the old Atocha
train station in Madrid included the
then-visionary "greening" of the area
under the wrought-iron and glass
roof (built 1888–92). Revamped by
Rafael Moneo in metal, glass and
polished stone, the space features an
indoor tropical garden where
travelers can sit on benches and enjoy
the lily pond and the regular misting
of the garden by tall, slender, metal-
stalked sprayers.

The spectacular plant at the center of
the picture is a giant bird-of-paradise.

PAGES 166–167

Columbia University

New York City. Designed by
Lynden B. Miller, 1999

Originally trained as an artist, Lynden
B. Miller specializes in public garden
design. Over the last twenty years,
she has transformed many of New
York City's parks and public spaces
with designs that enhance the city
dweller's sense of nature. Miller's
sensitive use of color and dedicated
plant knowledge translate into
gardens of outstanding beauty, like
this one at Columbia University. She
is active in restoration projects,
including those at Bryant Park,
Madison Square Park, the
Conservatory Garden in Central Park,
and various areas of the New York
Botanical Garden.

RIGHT
Marina Linear Park
San Diego, California. Designed by Martha Schwartz, 1998
Martha Schwartz is on the cutting edge of modern landscape architecture; her often humorous work combines land art, historical nuances and unusual materials. For Marina Linear Park, she created a strong link between the city of San Diego and its waterfront. While the park runs parallel to the old railroad yard, its sandy, winding paths break up the linear aspect, encouraging pedestrians to use a trail that's anything but straight.

PAGES 170–171
Ernsting's Family Campus
Coesfeld-Lette, Germany. Designed by Peter Wirtz, 2001
This elegant park was designed as a space to be viewed from the office workplaces surrounding it, and to give the employees of a German clothing retailer, Ernsting's Family, a place to relax. Peter Wirtz's landscape of organic curves and open areas lives harmoniously with David Chipperfield's functional architecture. The mounded grass hummocks, sensuous serpentine hedges and reflecting pool create an island of peace and calm.

PAGES 172–173
Shell Petroleum Headquarters
Rueil-Malmaison, France. Designed by Kathryn Gustafson, 1989–1991
Having outgrown its Paris offices, Shell decided to build a new corporate complex in a quiet neighborhood nineteen miles outside the city. Mindful of its residential location, Shell turned to landscape architect Kathryn Gustafson.

Her sensitive, lyrical solution for the site includes rolling berms to separate homes from the office campus, pocket gardens visible from every office window, and an on-site public garden. A ribbonlike aquatic garden, shown here, parallels both an outdoor walkway and an indoor glass-enclosed corridor. Its banks of flowering bushes have earned it the nickname "The Impressionist Garden."

PAGES 174–175
Toronto Music Garden
Toronto, Canada. Designed by Julie Moir Messervy with Yo-Yo Ma, 1999
At the waterfront Toronto Music Garden, designer Julie Moir Messervy and renowned cellist Yo-Yo Ma have interpreted Bach's "First Suite for Unaccompanied Cello" in nature. Each movement – Prelude, Allemande, Courante, Sarabande, Menuett and Gigue – corresponds to a section of the garden.

In the Prelude section, the music conjures the image of a flowing river – interpreted here in a curving streambed of granite rocks. Messervy suggests that the straight-trunked hackberry trees, with their regular spacing, resemble measures of music.

A Roof with a View

Roof gardens are wonderful spaces "in the air" that don't take up valuable real estate on the ground. Many businesses now utilize rooftop spaces, but roof gardens are much more commonly found as private gardens for entertaining and dining *al fresco*. Often the views are deliberately left open, offering dramatic visual perspectives – skyscapes instead of landscapes.

Schneider Roof Garden

This thousand-square-foot roof garden in New York City was designed for the Schneider family by Jeff Mendoza in 1995. The clients preferred to have full views of the surrounding city rather than to screen the space with trees. To accommodate that idea, Mendoza installed a low wall of shrubs, perennials and annuals that provides a sense of enclosure. Two columnar junipers act as a frame for the breathtaking city views.

Apex Garden

Occupying a prestigious site in the City of London, the No. 1 Poultry building was designed by James Stirling as an office with a rooftop restaurant. Arabella Lennox-Boyd added the half-acre Apex Garden to serve as a social space with amazing views of St. Paul's Cathedral and the city skyline. The garden's layout of boxwood was inspired by medieval "ridge and furrow" formations in plowed fields.

MILLENNIUM PARK

This great space in Chicago is a tribute to the city's motto *Urbs in Horto* (City in a Garden). Dramatically bordered by the skyscrapers of Michigan Avenue to the west and the blue expanse of Lake Michigan to the east, the location was originally flat marshland, and later, open railroad yard. Today, the park acts as a "green roof" over the still-operating railroad and underground parking.

Within Millennium Park, the 2½-acre Lurie Garden refers to Chicago's past, present and future via two distinct areas – the shady Dark Plate, representing Chicago's marshy past, and the Light Plate, an open-sun area that speaks to the city's present and future.

Jay Pritzker Pavilion

Renowned architect Frank Gehry engineered the outdoor pavilion, which is the summer home of Chicago's Grant Park Orchestra and Chorus. A web of steel pipes over the grassy area holds state-of-the-art sound equipment, so that every one of the seven thousand people gathered on the lawn can hear the music as clearly as the four thousand visitors seated under the pavilion's free-form roof.

In front of the pavilion, Piet Oudolf has assembled sweeps of sun-loving false indigo, betony, calamint and sea lavender, interspersed with grasses. About 65 percent of the twenty-six thousand plants in the park are native to this area.

BELOW

The Seam

Between the Light Plate and the Dark Plate is "The Seam" – a boardwalk lined by a low wall. It acts as both a division and a link – physically between the plates and metaphorically between the future and the past. The boardwalk itself traces the site of the old Lake Michigan seawall and is a reminder of Chicago's earliest "architecture" – the boardwalks that rose above the marshy, muddy streets. The limestone wall beside it is made of the same stone that lines Chicago's lakeshore.

PAGES 180–181

Lurie Garden

Chicago, Illinois. Designed by Kathryn Gustafson, Jennifer Guthrie, Shannon Nichol, Robert Israel and Piet Oudolf, 2004

The Lurie Garden in Millennium Park is outlined by the "Shoulder Hedge," a living wall of European beech, hornbeam and evergreens that gets its name from Carl Sandburg's beloved depiction of Chicago as the "City of the Big Shoulders." In ten to twenty years the hedge will be the size and shape of the steel framework that surrounds it.

The hedge protects broad, meadowlike sweeps of perennials and grasses, designed by Dutch plantsman Piet Oudolf. Peaking in fall, ornamental grasses and coneflowers wave in the winds off Lake Michigan.

MEDITERRANEAN GARDENS

Mediterranean climates are characterized by hot, dry summers and cool, wet winters. These conditions are found in countries all around the globe – not only on the shores of the Mediterranean, but also in California, Chile, the Cape region of South Africa, and southwest and southern Australia.

Mediterranean-type plants thrive in all of these regions, although specific local variations of altitude, proximity to the sea, and air circulation may affect their success. There are approximately twenty-five thousand plant species growing in the wild in these areas – and more than half of these occur nowhere else in the world.

HOT SUMMERS, COOL WINTERS

Mediterranean-type plants thrive in a hot dry summer and a cool winter with light rain. They are drought-tolerant, but require good drainage. Many of the broad-leaved evergreen shrubs have shiny, aromatic leaves or hairy, silvery leaves that help them survive in hot climates. Most of us are familiar with some Mediterranean-type plants, which include bulbs from South Africa, rock roses from the Mediterranean, creeping ground-cover plants from the California chaparral, and acacias from Australia.

Lebanon Garden

Designed by landscape architect Vladimir Djurovic, this garden on the coast in Lebanon has stunning views of the Mediterranean Sea. The garden reflects Djurovic's strongly architectural style and minimal use of plants. Here, the simple vertical lines of palm trees unite the house with the terraced pools of an outdoor courtyard. Water is the medium that links indoor and outdoor living throughout the property.

RIGHT
La Majorelle

The painter Jacques Majorelle (1886–1962) designed a nine-acre garden in Marrakech, Morocco. He decorated it with colorful mosaics and painted it cobalt blue and turquoise with contrasting brick-red floors. He turned the garden into a paradise with eighteen hundred cactus varieties, tropical flowers, ferns, bamboo groves and palm trees. The property was restored by fashion designer Yves Saint Laurent in 1981.

PAGES 186–187
Tresco Abbey Gardens

Isles of Scilly, United Kingdom. Designed by owner Augustus Smith and developed by the Smith family, 1834–present
At Tresco Abbey, off the coast of Cornwall, England, the Gulf Stream ensures a Mediterranean-type climate. Frosts are rare, but sea gales are frequent. In 1834, Augustus Smith established a shelter belt of Monterey pines on the property. Then he built terraced gardens in the ruins of the old abbey, where the slopes provide protection for a rare mix of plants from around the globe. Succulents, agaves, palms, cycads, echiums and the spectacular Mexican *Furcraea longaeva* thrive, improbably, just miles from the coast of England. Today the fourth generation of Smiths continues to care for the gardens.

La Mortella

Ischia, Italy. Designed by
Russell Page for Sir William
and Lady Walton;
developed by Lady Walton,
1956–present

The garden created for the
composer Sir William
Walton and his wife,
Susana, was originally
designed nearly fifty years
ago. Much of the garden
lies in a deep cleft filled
with rich alluvial soil – in
sharp contrast to the rest of
the garden, which hangs on
the dry rocky slopes above.

A passionate plantswoman,
Lady Walton has enriched
the garden with more than
one thousand rare and
exotic plant species.
Featuring Islamic-style
water rills and fountains,
the garden was recently
opened to the public.

RIGHT
La Casella

Grasse, France. Designed by owners Tom Parr and Claus Scheinert, 2000–present

This luxuriously planted garden in the south of France makes good use of the typical Mediterranean climate of cool winters and hot summers. Eight terraces, each with a different character, are set into a Provence hillside. On this terrace, background olive trees set the scene for plants from around the world. Bright blue California lilac from the United States, African daisy from South Africa, 'Bowles' Mauve' wallflower and many silver-leaved plants all thrive here.

PAGES 190–191
Villa Massei

Lucca, Tuscany, Italy. Designed by owners Gil Cohen and Paul Gervais, 1982–present

Set in the foothills of Monti Pisani in Tuscany, among oak, pine and chestnut woods, the garden around this sixteenth-century hunting lodge is a synthesis of old and new. Its current owners have re-created a stylish Italian Renaissance garden embellished with exciting plants, including an ancient camphor tree and a fruit-bearing jujube tree. Behind the house, a wisteria pergola, underplanted with ferns, leads to an original grotto where boxwood-edged beds encircle potted citrus trees.

TROPICAL
GARDENS

The true tropical or torrid zone covers almost a quarter of the world's surface. Many local conditions found in this zone can affect the choice of flora in a garden. With their understanding of these variable environmental conditions, designers like Roberto Burle Marx have raised tropical gardening to the level of an art form.

In the public realm, botanic gardens have become important repositories for tropical plant collections from around the world. Originally established by colonial powers, mainly for commercial reasons, tropical botanic gardens turned to more scientific pursuits in the early 1900s and are now valued institutions for plant study and research.

THE INFLUENCE OF ROBERTO BURLE MARX

The great garden designer Roberto Burle Marx was highly influential in encouraging the use of regional native plants. Working in Brazil, where he was deeply inspired by the natural surroundings, Burle Marx chose luxuriant, vividly colored tropical plants to create gardens that evoked the local landscape.

Crediting Burle Marx as his mentor, Miami landscape architect Raymond Jungles makes equally inspirational gardens in the Florida Keys, where tropical and subtropical zones merge. Plant options abound there, as the area's biodiversity is greater than anywhere else in the United States.

Raul de Souza Martins Garden

Many of the residential sites at which Roberto Burle Marx worked are located in the mountainous, forested areas outside Rio de Janeiro. In this hillside garden, built between 1983 and 1988, he used a series of terraces as a showcase for native flora. In this view toward the house, luxuriant bromeliads, shown in the foreground, spill over the edges of a walkway.

Raymond Jungles Garden

Raymond Jungles designed a lush
tropical garden in Key West, Florida,
with his wife, Deborah Yates. Here,
Jungles achieved clarity and simplicity
while using a wide range of plants.
Many of these come from Brazil, while
others are native to the Florida Keys.
The Satake palm tree is from the
Ryuku Islands near Japan.

The focal point of the garden is the
fountain, with its brilliant, abstract tile
mural designed by Roberto Burle
Marx and Haruyoshi Ono.

Cavanellas Garden

Petropolis, Brazil. Designed by Roberto Burle Marx, 1954

Roberto Burle Marx worked closely with architect Oscar Niemeyer at this property in the mountainous state of Rio de Janeiro. The house's curved roof and open floor plan led Burle Marx to design an equally simple, architectural garden. Bright squares of variegated St. Augustine grass alternate with a darker form of the grass. Taller squares of maroon bloodleaf plants and bright licorice plants add to the tiled effect. The bronze figure reclining in the landscape is the work of sculptor Alfredo Ceschiatti, who was working in Brazil at the same time as Burle Marx and Niemeyer.

The lawn's design proved difficult for the original owners to maintain over time, but the garden has been faithfully restored by the current owner.

BELOW

Monteiro

Correias, Brazil. Designed by Roberto Burle Marx for
Odette Monteiro, 1946

Monteiro is Roberto Burle Marx's most famous garden – and
the first landscape in which he planted native plants in great,
abstract sweeps. Seeking to re-create the look of the
surrounding natural landscape, he used regional plants in
nature-inspired patterns and broad brushstrokes of color.
Sweeps of bright cannas, coleus, bloodleaf plants and spider
plants line the winding drive in the spectacular valley.

PAGES 200–201

Sitio Santo Antonio da Bica

Guaratiba, Brazil. Designed by owner Roberto Burle Marx,
1949–85

Sitio Santo Antonio da Bica, outside the city of Rio de Janeiro,
was Roberto Burle Marx's own home, where he lived from 1949
until 1985. Here, Marx built his collection of Brazilian native
plants, of which he had an encyclopedic knowledge.

In order to create microclimates, he built greenhouses and
seed beds at different levels; bromeliads were grown in stone
structures like the one seen here. The range of plants is
extraordinary, from desert *Furcraea* to moisture-loving gingers.

PAGES 202–203

Fairchild Tropical Botanic Garden

Coral Gables, Florida. Designed by William Lyman Phillips,
1938–present

Robert Montgomery, a successful businessman with a passion
for plant collecting, founded the Fairchild Tropical Botanic
Garden in southern Florida in the 1930s. He named it in honor
of his friend the great botanist and plant explorer David
Fairchild, who established the collections, including significant
groupings of palms and cycads. Shown is one of the most
beautiful palms, blue-leaved *Bismarckia nobilis*, a Madagascar
native with striking fan-shaped leaves.

Today the garden helps to identify endangered plants
throughout the tropics, with an emphasis on research in
taxonomy and ethnobotany. Considerably damaged by
Hurricane Andrew in 1992, and again in the storms of 2004,
the collections are currently being restored.

PAGES 204–205

National Orchid Garden

Singapore Botanic Gardens, Singapore, 1995

The Singapore Botanic Gardens were established by Sir
Stamford Raffles as a trial plot for spice plants in 1822. They
were abandoned after his death. The present garden, founded
in 1859, was first a public park and then a site for experimental
crops such as coffee, cocoa, sugar and, in particular, the
commercially successful rubber plant.

The National Orchid Garden opened within the Singapore
Botanic Gardens in 1995; sixty thousand orchids are displayed
on its nearly eight acres of landscaped slopes. Various
Dendrobium orchid hybrids are shown here.

DESERT GARDENS

A garden design that uses very little water is called a xeriscape. Designers working with xeriscapes plan for water conservation, and must also study prevailing shade and sun patterns, wind flow and, of course, rainfall.

Plants with succulent, water-storing leaves or deep, water-searching roots work well in desert conditions. Known as xerophytes, these plants are naturally adaptable to low-fertility desert soils. Many xerophytes have unusual three-dimensional or sculptural shapes, which can bring startling beauty to the desert landscape.

NATURALLY DRY

Although gardeners in the North American desert must constantly consider water conservation, the shapely, textured gardens they create have a strange, alluring beauty. Plants are chosen for their drought tolerance as well as for their architectural shapes, gigantic flowering stems or unusual growth tendencies. Desert gardens are, naturally, minimalist gardens, where even the shadow of a plant can be a creative element in the landscape.

Kotoske Garden

This residential garden, designed by Steve Martino, is in Paradise Valley, near Phoenix, Arizona. With drought-resistant planting and simple, architectural forms, it exemplifies desert modernism. Massive blue-gray slabs make a geometric grid for specimen-filled borders. The pale yellow palo verde makes a strong statement in one corner, while octopus agave casts long afternoon shadows. The water cascade on the plum-colored wall adds just a touch of opulence to this minimalist setting.

Kitchell Garden

This desert garden in Paradise Valley, Arizona, takes full advantage of the view of Camelback Mountain. Designer John Douglas installed a central water feature – a noisy rill – which extends from the house to the garden's low wall. The flowing water offers a sense of contrast with the drought-tolerant xerophytic plants. Creosote, palo verde and ironwood trees, all of which grow on the slopes of the nearby mountain, blend with the golden hues of the natural desert landscape beyond the garden's perimeter.

Ruth Bancroft Garden

Walnut Creek, California. Designed by owner Ruth Bancroft, 1950–present
Ruth Bancroft's interest in desert plants began more than fifty years ago, with a gift of *Aeonium* 'Glenn Davidson'. This acquisition began a passion for desert plants, and by 1972 Bancroft's collection of succulents had expanded to include attractive sculptural specimens. They now fill her dry garden in the heart of northern California's fruit-growing area.

A pioneer in the xeriscape movement, Bancroft created a natural setting with the aid of Lester Hawkins from Western Hills Nursery. Amoeba-shaped beds and creeping ground-cover plants blur the lines of gravel paths. The collection of different agave plants contributes to the drama of the garden.

PAGES 212–213
Desert Garden

Huntington Botanical Gardens, San Marino, California. Designed by William Hertrich, 1928
In 1903, railroad magnate Henry E. Huntington developed a series of specialized plant collections around the Huntington Library building. Opening in 1928 as the Huntington Botanical Gardens, they included, in the Desert Garden, a world-famous collection of cacti and other xerophytic plants.

Significant groupings of agaves, aloes, and fantastical boojum trees mingle with succulent ground-cover plants, euphorbias, and five hundred golden barrel cacti (far right). A section called the Heritage Walk, which opened to the public in 2003, features some of the Desert Garden's oldest specimens.

MATERIALS MATTER

In the last fifty years, landscape architects and garden designers, often in collaboration with artists and sculptors, have taken traditional materials such as wood, glass and stone into new territory. Some materials are "discovered" after being recycled. Others are new composite materials from industrial sources, which have expanded the vocabulary of design.

Always, the trick is to use the properties of the material in an innovative way – whether it is molded, chipped, polished, carved or twisted.

FIRE & WATER

Architect Vladimir Sitta is a designer who uses materials in new, unexpected ways. In his designs, gardens are associated with their surroundings, past and present. He stresses a theme of "eternity," using the most elemental and ancient of materials – fire and water – for his thoughtful settings.

RIGHT
Theatre of Lights

This small courtyard garden in Sydney, Australia, is enclosed by terra cotta walls. In it, four slabs of black marble – Sitta calls them "wells" – are supported by thick pieces of sand-blasted glass that rest in chips of crushed green marble. The black slabs are covered in a film of light-reflecting water. Fiber optic lighting cables, plus sound and misting equipment, are housed in a chamber below.

At night, a controlled sound and light show begins – hence the name "Theatre of Lights." Programmed mists float upward, swirling around the bamboos' stems and enveloping the garden in "clouds."

LEFT
Fire Garden

Vladimir Sitta's Fire Garden in Sydney seeks to reconnect a modern Australian garden with the ancient Australian landscape. Historically, the ecosystem was managed by Aborigines, and was dependent on periodic fires to induce germination and new vegetation. Now, the use of fire evokes a time and place well beyond the boundaries of the garden. This idea brings the silent history of the Australian landscape to life – in a suburban backyard.

LEFT
Antony

Cornwall, England. Fountain designed by William Pye, 1996

William Pye is a world-renowned specialist in sculptural water designs.
He uses materials such as stainless steel to give shape and form to water.
Pye's inspiration came from watching a thin film of rain running down a road in
rhythmic patterns. He realized that water can be directed and energized in
infinite ways – pumped, dripped, poured and splashed – for dramatic effect.

At Antony, Pye rethought the notion of a fountain, fashioning bronze into a cone
shape that mimics the adjacent topiary yews. Water drips down the patterned
surface, shimmering as it falls.

PAGES 220–221
Garstons

Isle of Wight, England. Designed by owner Jenny Jones, 1995

At her farmhouse on the Isle of Wight, Jenny Jones designed a garden that
reflects the sense of high visual drama she acquired during her career in theater
design. Here, she planned a series of glass walls and prisms, originally intended to
enclose clumps of bamboo and to prevent wind funnels. The see-through glass
reflects the calm water of the nearby square garden pool – but it distorts the
reflections, adding mystery and confusion to the scene. Jones's interest in how
materials change in different lights has led to an unusual visual interplay.

PAGES 222–223
Canada Garden

Tokyo, Japan. Designed by Shunmyo Masuno, 1993

The Canada Garden at the Canadian Embassy in Tokyo is on the building's fourth
floor. The intent was to create a garden symbolic of Canada, yet true to the spirit
of Japanese culture. Designed by a Zen priest, Shunmyo Masuno, the only living
ishidateso, or priest-designer, it is composed in the Japanese tradition, with raked
gravel and rocks representing ocean waves and islands.

Visitors "travel" past a pond (the Atlantic Ocean), granite stones (the Canadian
Shield), three pyramidal stones (the Canadian Rockies) and a second water
feature (the Pacific Ocean) before they reach the Japanese garden shown here.

PAGES 224–225
San Francisco Garden

San Francisco, California. Designed by Topher Delaney, 2004

In her design for a small sanctuary garden, Topher Delaney chose unusual
materials and surfaces to suggest sky and water. Varying tones of blue
Marmorino plaster make up the walls, and the panels are separated by bands of
stainless steel. The blues echo the colors of nearby San Francisco Bay.

In this minimalist garden, everything is functional. A scalloped marble screen
from India – called a *chadar* – serves as a fountain, refreshing the space and
muffling city noises.

RECYCLED & "FOUND"

Both natural and manmade materials can have a second life in the garden.
The imaginative and resourceful use of local materials – sea shells, driftwood and local stone – can
lead to garden statements that are just as profound as the choice of native plants. Rubber tires used as
stepping stones or recycled beer barrels used as ornamental plant containers can astonish with their
obvious functionality and unexpected beauty. All express environmental economy instead of the
extravagance of new, more expensive materials, which can waste the world's resources.

Mien Ruys Garden

The influential Dutch designer Mien Ruys, who died in 1998, was in the forefront of ecological gardening. This pond is in one of the model gardens at the famous Moorheim nursery , at Dedemsvaart in the Netherlands, where she created low-maintenance designs with hardy plants. Few herbicides and synthetic fertilizers were used. These model gardens continue to provide the public with a chance to study ecological principles that they can use in their own gardens. For this pond Ruys recycled rubber tires into stepping stones.

Lotusland

At Lotusland in Montecito, California, the much-married opera singer Ganna Walska created an extraordinary garden stage set, beginning in 1941. Eccentric and strange, colorful and weird, the garden's design is held together by Walska's vision. It is an inventive mix of materials, where water, rocks and shells – including giant clam shells – mingle with some of the world's most unusual species of cacti, cycads, succulents and palms.

Madoo

Sagaponack, New York. Designed by owner Robert Dash, 1967–present

Artist Robert Dash has designed his own dramatic garden on the east end of Long Island. He uses traditional materials in unusually sophisticated ways. A gently curving pathway is composed of tree trunk slices set in rough gravel. Lined with boxwood and white impatiens, the path exemplifies Dash's understated style.

The garden constantly surprises. Step, door and window colors change throughout the year, and plants are rethought seasonally to maximize visual impact. The garden's name, Madoo, comes from an old Scottish way of saying "my dove."

GLASS IN THE GARDEN

Landscape designer Andy Cao spent his childhood in Vietnam, and this environment has influenced much of his work. For his own garden in the hills of Los Angeles, he drew on iconic elements from Vietnamese culture to create a stylized landscape. Cao assembled crushed and tumbled glass into a reproduction of the patchwork of rice terraces, banana groves, and surreal-looking salt farms that he recalled. Recycled glass, with its many color possibilities, proved to be an economical, innovative material for his very modern designs.

Desert Sea

The Desert Sea was designed in 2001 for the theatrical environment of the Chaumont-sur-Loire Festival in France. It was inspired by both African body decoration and Vietnamese water puppets. Materials Cao used for this installation included seven miles of Manila rope, ten tons of cobalt blue glass, crushed plate glass, and four tons of industrial marbles as a bed for a bamboo grove.

Glass Garden

Cao's own Glass Garden is a strange, contained landscape that re-creates scenes from his memory in an unlikely place far from his childhood home. It places particular emphasis on his memories of the salt mounds of Vietnam. Eleven "salt" heaps form the core of the garden. They appear to float in the still, dark water, glowing, ghostly, in the moonlight.

BELOW
Glass Garden

Andy Cao's experimenting for his Glass Garden began with a single bucket of crushed glass. Recycled glass in five different colors provides beds for succulents and other tropical plants, including bananas and agaves.

PAGES 232–233
Glass Garden

Los Angeles, California.
Designed by Andy Cao, 1998

The heart of the Glass Garden is the reflecting pond, with floating mounds that recall the salt-farming scenes of Cao's youth. These strange white mounds, the bright blue crushed and tumbled glass "flower" beds and the strong architectural shapes of agaves create a magical landscape. A lavender-colored wooden wall is a modernist touch.

LongHouse Reserve

East Hampton, New York. Installation by Dale Chihuly, 2000
Dale Chihuly studied interior design and architecture in the
early 1960s, but has since become enthralled by glass-blowing.
Now he uses argon, neon and blown glass to create colorful
sculptures. This installation, *Cobalt Blue Reeds*, is located by the
lotus pool at the LongHouse Reserve. Belonging to textile
designer Jack Lenor Larsen, the garden is now open to the public
and is the site of many modern works of art, often in vibrantly
colored or unusual materials.

INDIVIDUAL
VISION

*Many of today's landscape architects and garden
designers choose to work in a vernacular style local to
their region or country; others transform old ideas
with new materials and techniques.
All of the best bring an awareness of the
environment to their work.*

*Modern designers, however different their styles,
still see the garden as a refuge for the spirit and
a balm for the soul.*

CUES FROM THE CULTURE

Many of the best contemporary designers have developed distinctive styles that have
strong overtones of their native cultures. The Spanish landscape architect Fernando Caruncho,
originally a classical philosopher, has been inspired by a relationship between Moorish-Spanish
architecture and the history of the land and its agriculture. His quite formal style uses
water features in highly visual grid systems.

Juan Grimm works in the wilder, more scenic landscape of coastal Chile. In his naturalistic designs,
evergreen shrubs and native plants blend seamlessly into the mountainous landscape.

Cotoner

Fernando Caruncho created
this garden on the
Mediterranean island of
Majorca in 1991–2. It
complements a modern
house designed by the
owner in a traditional
farmhouse style . The
garden is divided into a grid
of sixteen squares lined
with alternating Italian
cypress and olive trees. The
four corners of the plan are
planted with oleanders,
while the two squares
immediately in front of
the house are evergreen
Pistacia lentiscus, a
resinous shrub native to the
Mediterranean. The focal
point is a lake with an
irregular outline. Caruncho's
love of geometry and
formal use of native plants
unite the entire garden.

Bahía Azul Garden

Juan Grimm, Chile's most distinguished landscape architect, has positioned his own garden on the spectacular northern coast of Chile, high above the cliffs. The garden's undulating paths descend toward the sea and to a swimming pool that nestles in the rocks at the ocean's edge. Grimm uses native plants as well as plants from similar Mediterranean-type climates for his naturalistic effects. House and garden seem to merge into the landscape.

BELOW
Ayrlies

Auckland, New Zealand. Designed by owner
Beverly McConnell, 1964–present

Beverly McConnell began her garden at Ayrlies
nearly fifty years ago; since then, her vision has
continued to evolve. In her painterly garden,
McConnell uses the combination of acidic soil
and high rainfall to her advantage. It allows for
an incredibly wide range of plants from many
continents. Groves of trees – many of North
American origin – lead to a luxuriant valley of
native tree ferns. Where drainage is adequate,
South African bulbs and shrubs thrive among
palm and fig trees. Waterfalls, green lawns and
clematis-covered pergolas contribute to the
naturalistic style.

PAGES 242–243
Broughton Grange

Oxfordshire, England. Designed by
Tom Stuart-Smith, 2000

At Broughton Grange, the talented English designer Tom Stuart-Smith has created a garden where formality is softened by the fine, naturalistic planting for which he is acclaimed. Stuart-Smith is a knowledgeable plantsman who can manipulate space brilliantly.

By terracing this garden, he dramatically extends the feeling of space. The middle terrace, shown here, is an open area with a square pond. To one side is a heavily planted lower terrace – but from this vantage point one looks past the topiaries and out to the landscape beyond.

PAGES 244–245
Heveningham Hall

Suffolk, England. Designed by
Kim Wilkie, 1995

The original garden for the eighteenth-century Heveningham Hall was designed by Capability Brown, who died before the project could be implemented. Two hundred years later, English landscape architect Kim Wilkie has reinterpreted the plans that Brown left behind. On the south side of the house, where the land rises sharply, what was once a Victorian parterre is now an expanse of spectacular curving grass terraces. Flowing away from the house, the terraces fan outward toward the ancient trees on the site.

OUTSIDE ARTISTS

Modern designers often employ technical innovations and exotic ideas in their gardens. Both Vladimir Sitta and artist César Manrique use history as a theme in their work. Sitta's garden designs respond to the pressures of modern life, but still possess an ancient, elemental quality. Manrique's artistic vision salutes an island garden's volcanic history in an unusual and dramatic way.

Jardín de Cactus

In an old volcanic quarry in the natural cactus fields on the island of Lanzarote, in the Canary Islands, César Manrique carved out the Jardín de Cactus. Laid out between 1987 and 1992, the garden is shaped like a giant amphitheater. Ten thousand specimens of cacti, in all shapes and sizes, grow on the terraces, which are punctuated by volcanic stone sculptures. One of Manrique's modern sculptures, a twenty-six-foot green metal cactus, marks the garden's entrance.

RIGHT
Garangula

Vladimir Sitta's vision for Garangula takes into account the historic origins of this 1850s homestead in New South Wales, Australia. It includes the dramatic Folly Cone, sculpted from rough granite stones and crowned by "hairs" of twisted copper rods. At the cone's base, Sitta cut a jagged stream in the paving that leads to the swimming pool. At night, the press of a button lights jets in the cone, emitting water vapor, which drifts out into the garden.

PAGES 248–249
Garangula

Heuden, New South Wales, Australia.
Designed by Vladimir Sitta,
1989–present
Located in the area called South Western Slopes, Garangula was once a working farm. The owners called upon Vladimir Sitta to create a new garden plan as the homestead was being restored. Sitta designed the main terrace, seen here, as a more formal transition between the house and a lower area of old-growth trees. A path with two types of grass leads to clipped hedges, wide stairs and terraces for displaying art, such as the round sculpture in the distance.

An Architect's Eye

Christopher Bradley-Hole was originally an architect. He set up his own landscape
practice in 1996 and proceeded to triumph with his designs for London's Chelsea Flower Show.
Based on pure geometry, his designs eliminate unnecessary clutter in favor of open spaces,
modern streamlined materials and sustainable planting. His passion for perennials makes his
rather austere, minimalist layouts seem comfortable and welcoming.

Old Rectory

Christopher Bradley-
Hole's love of geometry is
in clear evidence at this
circular stone
amphitheater in the
countryside of Sussex,
England. The double-
walled circle was
meticulously laid by
craftsmen who specialize
in drystone walling. The
amphitheater is at the
back of the property,
behind the Georgian-
style house.

Thoresen-Macklin Garden

The London rooftop garden that
Christopher Bradley-Hole designed for
Gail Thoresen and Tim Macklin is a place
for a quiet meal – and an outstanding
view. The central deck of red cedar is
surrounded by galvanized steel planters
in various shapes and sizes, all filled with
tall grasses. Dwarf Japanese pines edge
the terrace and act as a windbreak.

PAGES 252–253

Fawler Copse

Berkshire, England. Designed by
Christopher Bradley-Hole, 2003

Christopher Bradley-Hole describes his
designs as having "a sense of space
through abstract geometry." His work
often begins with a rigidly geometric
layout. He then disguises the bones of
the plan with luxuriant, soft plantings
that blur the straight lines.

At this new, timber-framed house, a vast,
oak-boarded terrace descends into the
garden via shallow steps. The formal beds
are pocket-sized for ease of maintenance.
This terrace and the one at the front of
the house anchor the home within the
surrounding landscape.

The Garden of Cosmic Speculation

In 1989 architect Charles Jencks and his wife, Maggie Keswick, took their first steps toward building a thematic garden at their home at Portrack in southwest Scotland. Over the next few years their joint creative efforts led to the development of the garden that, after Maggie's death in 1995, would come to be called the Garden of Cosmic Speculation.

In this thought-provoking garden, Jencks uses landforms, water, rocks, plants and artwork to speculate on the deeper ideas and laws underlying nature. Each of the main areas of the garden is devoted to a fundamental discovery of our time: black holes, fractals in nature, DNA, evolutionary "jumps," and the basic units of the universe. Although the garden's design stems from recent discoveries, it is not a science lesson; rather, it is a sensory exploration of the basic principles that guide the universe.

Landforms & Lakes

Landforms are at the heart of the Garden of Cosmic Speculation. They are the most pronounced contours in the garden and give terrestrial shape to cosmic themes: waves, curves, fractal patterns and the spiral of the double helix.

An aerial photograph shows the main landforms as they appear today. As soil was removed to form the lakes, it was reshaped into dimensional wave patterns: Snake Mound (above) and Snail Mound (below).

Black Hole Terrace

Although the term "black hole" was not used until 1967, the idea of an invisible star was first suggested in the 1790s. A black hole is an area of space that is so matter-compressed that nothing can escape it. A black hole's supergravity rips space apart and swallows matter and light – hence its blackness.

Scientists theorize that every galaxy may have at its center a rotating black hole with a plasma jet of electrons shooting out in both directions. Jencks transforms the idea of a plasma jet and spinning galaxy into a garden seat (shown at left). Food is brought here for dining, or one can simply sit and ponder the view.

DNA Garden

Before its latest incarnation, the DNA Garden was first a kitchen garden, then a physics garden, and then a garden of the six senses. Each layer built upon the other. The original grid layout was partly based on the Scottish family tartan of Maggie Keswick, Jencks's wife.

The sixth sense, intuition, is traditionally considered a feminine sense. It is represented by a sculpture of a woman (shown below); she looks at her brain as receptor-fingers gather information.

Universe Cascade

The Universe Cascade, at the center of the garden, is the culmination of all the ideas – and paths – leading to it. The twenty-five major "jumps" in the universe's development are indicated by abrupt turns in the stairs' direction.

In this extraordinary view of the Universe Cascade, looking down the steps from the top, twists and spirals repeat the wave motif used throughout the garden. At Jump 11 (center left), the solar system forms. Jump 13 (center right) represents the moon's creation – an event that causes the seasons. Near left is Jump 15, where two spirals intersect at a green rock – and Gaia, the earth, begins to "breathe."

Snail Mound & Tail of the Snail

The Garden of Cosmic Speculation. Designed by Charles Jencks, 1989–present

Built in the form of a double helix, Snail Mound was shaped by several ideas: François I's sixteenth-century spiral stairway at Chambord; Egyptian ziggurats; the pavement maze at Chartres Cathedral; and, most obviously, the twin spiral of DNA. The "tail of the snail" is a French curve or hook that creates a path to the center of the lake below.

Curves and counter-curved shapes appear throughout the garden, mimicking waveforms that are often found in nature, such as the natural meandering of a river valley or the sand ridges on an ocean beach.

PAGES 258–259
Black Hole Terrace

The Garden of Cosmic Speculation. Designed by Charles Jencks, 1989–present

Walk on to the Black Hole Terrace and gravity pulls you downward – thus the garden uses the main force of nature physically, as well as symbolically. Photographs from the Hubble Space Telescope have revealed that supermassive black holes have a plasma jet at their center. At the Black Hole Terrace, a plasma jet sculpture becomes a backrest for an outdoor seat and a climbing frame for plants. Sign and symbol are merged.

PAGES 260–261
DNA Garden

The Garden of Cosmic Speculation. Designed by Charles Jencks, 1989–present

The DNA Garden reminds us that each sense is capable of "translating the language of the universe – energy waves – into the language of the nervous system – electrical impulses," according to Jencks. The aerial view of the DNA Garden shows six "cells," each with a double helix at its center. Counterclockwise from upper right are the senses of hearing, sight, touch, taste and smell. In the foreground is the sixth sense, the sense of intuition.

PAGES 262–263
Universe Cascade

The Garden of Cosmic Speculation. Designed by Charles Jencks, 1989– present

The Universe Cascade is built into the hill that drops below Portrack House. One "climbs" through thirteen billion years of cosmic history. At the top is the future, while at the base, before time and space existed, is the unity of matter and energy. A series of landforms represents universes unlike our own. In the foreground, a "membrane" universe, with its curving landform, brings the visitor to the first steps of the Cascade. Since it is not possible to know the universe's first moment, the steps emerge from murky water.

In the Universe Cascade, water runs down while time runs up. Water spills from a tank located at the top; the structure there represents the future. At the bottom, water drives a fountain that spins nine "little universes" – seen here churning up foam as they turn.

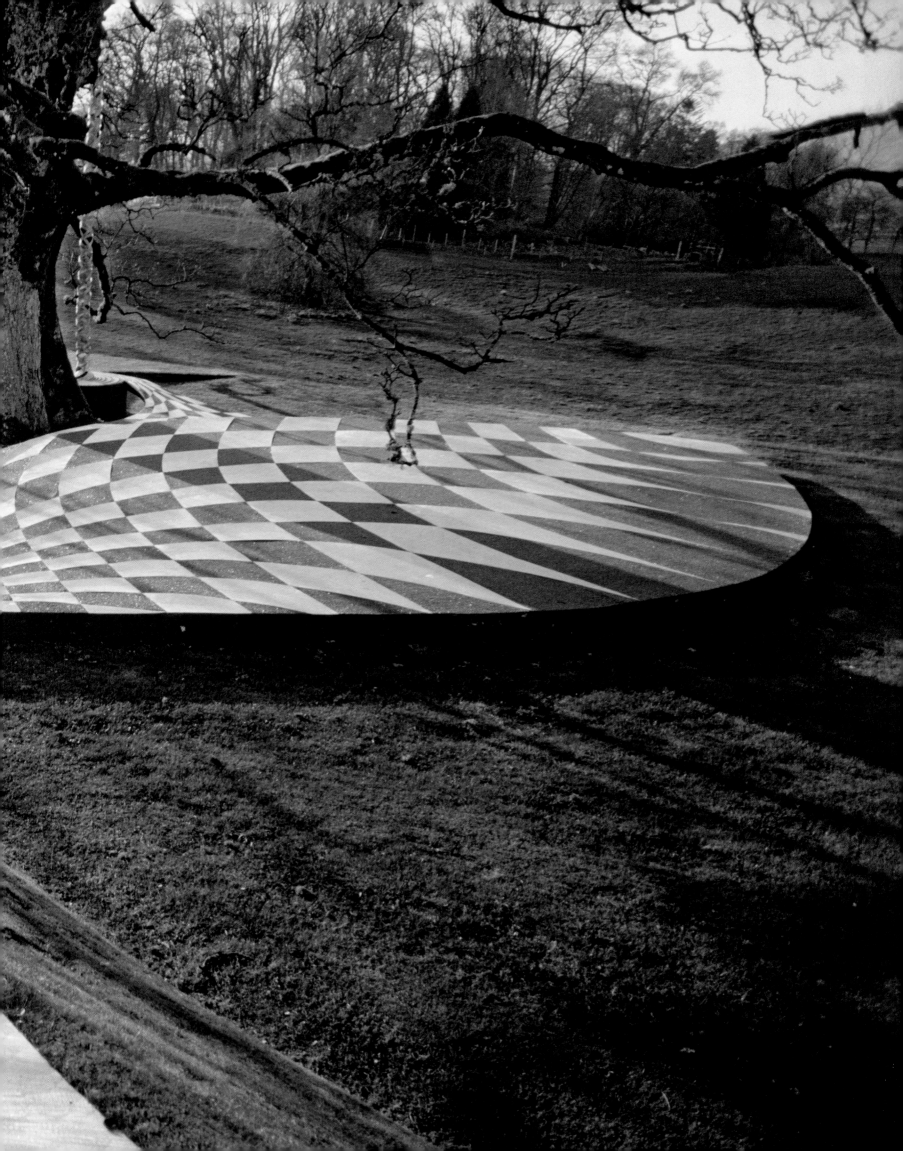

INDEX

A view to Evening Island, Chicago Botanic Garden. Evening Island designed by Oehme, van Sweden & Associates, Inc., 2002

PHOTOGRAPHIC ACKNOWLEDGMENTS

For permission to reproduce the photographs, paintings and archive material on the following pages the Publishers thank those listed below.

Sam Abell, National Geographic Image Collections: 24–5, 36
AKG-images/Bildarchiv Monheim: 72–3
Art Resource, New York © Alinari: 47 below
Art Resource, New York © Réunion des Musées Nationaux: 61
Art Resource, New York © Werner Forman Archive: 28–9
John Bethell © Garden Picture Library: 48–9
Bibliothèque nationale de France: 26
William Biderbost © Chicago Botanic Garden: 9, 267
Robert Emmett Bright: 46, 47 above
© The Trustees of the British Museum: 14
Judith Bromley: 119
Don Brown/www.chicagopictures.net: 6 below left, 179
Thomas A. Brown: 62–3
Nicola Browne: 124, 126–7, 132, 138–9, 142–3, 146, 150–51, 152, 155, 156–7, 163 below, 169, 172–3, 208, 231, 232–3
Linda Oyama Bryan: 270–71
Andrew Butler © National Trust Photographic Library: 5 below left, 80
Charlie Cobeen © Desert Botanical Garden: 159
Keith Collie © AKG London: 117 above
Topher Delaney: 2–3
John Feltwell/Garden Matters: 114–15
Roger Foley: 116
Georg Gerster: 15 above
Mick Hales: 10, 23, 78–9, 84–5, 94–5, 105 below, 122–3, 227
Jerry Harpur: 6 above left, 6 below right, 7 above right, 7 below right, 20–21, 30, 88, 128, 129, 130–31, 134, 136, 140–41, 144, 145 above, 158, 166–7, 170–71, 174–5, 176, 184, 188, 189, 192–3, 194, 195, 197, 200–201, 202–3, 204–5, 209, 214–15, 220–21, 224–5, 229, 235, 236–7, 247, 248–9, 251, 252–3
Derek Harris: 186–7
Marijke Heuff: 74–5, 226
Saxon Holt: 105 above, 108–9, 110–11, 117 below
Hakudo Inoue: 34–5

© James Iska: 118
Charles Jencks: 254, 255 above, 260–61
Andrea Jones/www.gardenexposures.com: 198–9, 210–11
Medhi Khansari: 12–13, 16
Balthazar Korab: 102–3, 112–13, 120–1,
Michèle Lamontagne © Garden Picture Library: 99 left
Michael Latz: 163 above
Andrew Lawson: 6 above right, 52–3, 96–7, 135, 147, 148–9, 177, 182–3, 190–91, 218, 222–3, 242–3, 250
Alain Le Toquin: 36–7, 66–7, 68–9, 70–71, 76–7, 162, 164–5, 185, 240–41, 246, 255 centre, 255 below, 256–7, 258–9
Allan Mandell © Portland Classical Chinese Garden: 27
Paolo Marton © Magnus Edizioni, S.p.A: 50–1
Nick Meers © Garden Picture Library: 82–3
Nick Meers © National Trust Photographic Library: 98, 100–101
© Middleton Place, Charleston, South Carolina: 5 below right, 104
Martine Mouchy © Garden Picture Library: 64–5
Clive Nichols: 7 above left, 59, 206–7, 212–13
Clive Nichols © Garden Picture Library: 91
North Wind Picture Archives: 60
Jean-Louis Nou © AKG London: 18–19
Paisajes Españoles © Fernando Caruncho and Associates: 238
Hugh Palmer: 153
Hugh Palmer © Red Cover: 4
Gary Rogers: 76 left, 86–7, 90, 106–7, 230
The Royal Collection © 2006, Her Majesty Queen Elizabeth II: 81
Ian Shaw © National Trust Photographic Library: 99 right
Vladimir Sitta: 216–7
Mark Tomaras © Millenium Park: 160–61, 178, 180–81
V&A Picture Library, Victoria and Albert Museum: 15 below
Guy Wenborne © Juan Grimm: 239
© Kim Wilkie: 244–5
Tobias Wittig: 31 below
Steven Wooster: 145 below
George Wright: 5 above right, 44–5, 54, 55, 56–7, 93
Michael S. Yamashita: 5 above left, 31 above, 32–3, 40–1, 42–3

PAGES 270–271
Evening Island, Chicago Botanic
Garden. Designed by Oehme, van
Sweden & Associates, Inc., 2002